Plate 175.

The Bay Tree.

Eliz. Blackwell delin. sculp. et Pinx.

1. Flower.
2. Fruit.
3. Fruit open.
4. Kernell.

Laurus.

A Celebration of Herbs

RECIPES FROM THE
HUNTINGTON HERB GARDEN

CONTRIBUTED BY HUNTINGTON STAFF,
SCHOLARS, AND VOLUNTEERS

BASED ON THE LECTURES OF
Shirley Kerins

SUPERVISING EDITOR
Peggy Park Bernal

EDITED BY
Judith Herman
AND
Jean Patterson

HUNTINGTON LIBRARY
San Marino, California

Published by the Huntington Library Press

1151 Oxford Road, San Marino, California 91108

www.huntington.org

Library of Congress Cataloging-in-Publication Data

A celebration of herbs : recipes from the Huntington herb garden /

contributed by Huntington staff, scholars, and volunteers ;

based on the lectures of Shirley Kerins ; supervising editor,

Peggy Park Bernal ; edited by Judith Herman and Jean Patterson.

p. cm.

Includes bibliographical references and index.

ISBN 0-87328-199-3 (hardcover : alk. paper)

1. Cookery (Herbs) 2. Herbs.

I. Kerins, Shirley II. Bernal, Peggy Park

III. Henry E. Huntington Library and Art Gallery.

TX819.H4 C45 2002

641.6'57—dc21

2002010504

Cover image from *The Good Hvswifes lewell* by Thomas Dawson, 1587.

Used by permission of the Huntington Library.

Printed in China

CONTENTS

ABOUT THE ILLUSTRATIONS

The twenty-four color plates of plants in this book were selected from among five hundred color drawings in Elizabeth Blackwell's *A Curious Herbal,* published in England in 1737. A copy of the two-volume book is in the Huntington's rare book collection. The book was intended to be a reference for doctors, and the text, drawn from Joseph Miller's *Botanicum Officinale,* which was printed in 1722, includes brief descriptions of the plants and their medicinal properties.

Born in Scotland, Mrs. Blackwell eloped to London with Andrew Blackwell, her second cousin. After a short apprenticeship, he opened a printing shop. However, at that time, a much longer apprenticeship was required to become a printer and, as a result, Mr. Blackwell was charged a heavy fine. The Blackwells could not pay the fine, so he was imprisoned.

Fortunately, Mrs. Blackwell learned of the need for a medical botany book and thought if she produced one, she could raise enough money to pay her husband's fine. She began work on the project with support from members of the Royal College of Physicians. She gathered live plants for models from the Chelsea Physic Garden near her home, which was founded in 1673 as the Apothecaries' Garden for the purpose of training apprentices in identifying plants. Mrs. Blackwell not only did the drawings, but she also etched the copper plates and colored the prints herself. This was considered a major accomplishment at the time because most botanical prints were created by three different artists—a sketcher, an engraver, and a painter. She produced the herbal in weekly parts for 125 weeks. Each part contained four copper-engraved plates with text, and her husband assisted with the text from his prison cell, writing it in several languages. The drawings were so accurate that a letter signed by several apothecaries recommending it was published in 1735.

Upon publication, the book proved to be immensely popular and a financial success. Most important for Mrs. Blackwell, the income from the sale of the book enabled her to pay her husband's debts and secure his release from prison. Ultimately, he seems to have been a bit of a ne'er-do-well because he was later forced to resign as Director of Improvements for the Duke of Chandos, and still later he was executed in Sweden for interfering with the royal succession.

She, however, was more successful. After her husband's death, she studied obstetrics and became a wealthy and successful general practitioner. And today, herb enthusiasts are still attracted by the charm of her engravings. Sixty copies of *A Curious Herbal* are known to survive in libraries around the world.

A CURIOUS HERBAL,

Containing

FIVE HUNDRED CUTS,

of the most useful Plants,

which are now used in the Practice of

PHYSICK.

Engraved on folio Copper Plates,
after Drawings, taken from

the LIFE.

By

Elizabeth Blackwell.

To which is added
a short Description of y'' Plants;
and
their common Uses in PHYSICK.

Vol: I.

LONDON

Printed for JOHN NOURSE *at the Lamb without*
Temple Bar. MDCCXXXIX.

THE HUNTINGTONS

Their Books and Their Gardens

Henry Edwards and Arabella Huntington, leading philanthropists of the early twentieth century, created an extraordinary educational and cultural institution in Southern California. He was a legendary book, art, and plant collector and a visionary leader in the development of greater Los Angeles. She was one of the wealthiest women in the nation at the turn of the twentieth century and an important art collector.

His money came from the railroads, urban streetcars, the utilities, and land development in Southern California, while she inherited her money from her first husband, Collis Huntington (also Henry's uncle), one of California's "big four" railroad developers. The couple divided their time between a mansion in New York, a chateau in France, and their estate in San Marino, in the San Gabriel Valley adjacent to Pasadena. She preferred New York and he preferred California—he fell in love with the valley the first time he saw it.

When they were in residence in San Marino, Mr. Huntington traveled to his office in downtown Los Angeles in a private railroad car. Meanwhile, Mrs. Huntington kept busy not only with household matters but also with weightier concerns, including the purchase of art for their growing collection of portraits by British painters Thomas Gainsborough, Joshua Reynolds, and Thomas Lawrence.

Interested in developing the grounds of his estate, Mr. Huntington experimented with rare plants to determine which ones adapted well to the mild Southern California climate. He visited local nurseries and plantsmen with his ranch superintendent, William Hertrich, in search of botanical rarities, and he assembled a variety of plant collections, including succulents, cactus, palms, cycads, and landmark trees, which can be seen in the Huntington Botanical Gardens today.

The institution's historic records do not reveal whether the Huntingtons had an herb garden, although herbs were probably grown in one of the six small greenhouses erected to plant vegetables: tomatoes, okra, string beans, cucumbers, melons, and summer squash. Although these vegetables were available at the market in nearby Pasadena, Mrs. Huntington wanted the ranch to supply everything, if possible, that was used in her kitchen.

Beyond vegetables, the varieties of fruit Mrs. Huntington had to choose from were mind-boggling. Not only did the family fruit orchard contain grapefruit and orange trees, but also tangerines, mandarin and blood oranges, kumquats, figs, apricots, nectarines, eight varieties of peaches, six varieties of plums, plus cherries, walnuts, sapotas, cherimoyas, guavas, and all manner of berries! And, of course, avocados should be mentioned because Mr. Huntington planted Southern California's first avocado orchard and the trees still bear fruit today.

For meat, the Huntingtons preferred poultry from their own yard. From March to July of 1916 a record of the consumption of poultry and eggs by family and servants showed that they consumed 554 dozen eggs, 437 chickens, 24 turkeys, 63 ducks, 23 guinea hens, and 159 squabs. A herd of Guernseys and a small dairy on the ranch provided dairy products as well.

The Huntington's Rare Herbals and Recipe Books

In 1910, at the age of sixty, Mr. Huntington began to concentrate on his lifelong love of books. His ambition was to build a preeminent research library with collections that would concentrate on British and American history and literature. He bought rare manuscripts and first editions of books at a rapid rate, sometimes purchasing entire libraries, occasionally at record prices.

The books were assembled in New York, where Mr. Huntington had a large apartment. As soon as the library building was completed in San Marino in 1921, railroad cars of books began to arrive at the ranch, where they were cataloged and made available for study by scholars.

Although botanical, horticultural, and recipe books were not among his chief interests, many valuable books of this kind were included in Mr. Huntington's *en bloc* purchases of private libraries. Among the botanical gems in the collection are Pierre Joseph Redouté's *Les Roses,* which contains the most outstanding depictions of roses ever made; the elephant folios of *Reichenbachia,* the greatest illustrated work on orchids; and several choice color-plate works on camellias. The collection also includes Linnaeus's *Species Plantarum,* the most important botanical book ever published, along with milestone publications in botany by such other major figures as De Candolle, Plumier, Bonpland, and Jussieu.

Herbals

Among the botanical books is a collection of about two hundred herbals, books that describe and illustrate plants used for medicine and flavorings, dating from the fifteenth to the eighteenth centuries. Because of their comments on everyday life, herbals are of interest to social historians, folklorists, botanists, and philologists. Social historians could make much of this comment, for example, in *The Grete Herbal* (1526), in which the author states that bathing is a strange, new fad and that "many folke that hathe bathed in cold water dyed." He also says that water drinking is equally pernicious!

The Huntington has many of the most notable herbals, including the following:

New Kreuterbuch (Basel, 1543; second edition and German translation of *De Historia Stirpium*) by Leonhart Fuchs (1501–1570). Fuchs was a true field botanist and the more than five hundred woodblock illustrations for his herbals were based on studies of living plants. The artist was Albrecht Meyer and his drawings were not of idealized specimens—some of the plants were drawn with broken stems and insect-eaten leaves. Nearly all of the illustrations in the subsequently famous sixteenth-century Flemish, English, and Swiss herbals were printed from these same woodblocks or copied from the illustrations in Fuchs's works.

New Herball (Cologne, 1568) by William Turner (1510–1568). Turner, the "Father of British Botany," holds the distinction of writing the only original botanical work written by an Englishman in the sixteenth century. The *New Herball* describes over two hundred species native to England, many of which were first named and discussed by him. Nearly all of the illustrations are from Fuchs's *De Historia Stirpium.*

Five Hundred Points of Good Husbandry (London, 1580) by Thomas Tusser (1515–1580). Tusser was the best known of sixteenth-century English writers who advised others on how to increase their yield and manage their property. Written in rhyming couplets, his book was the forerunner of what we know today as farmers' almanacs. It was in such demand that thirteen editions were printed over the next twenty-five years.

The Herball, or General Historie of Plants (London, 1597) by John Gerard (1545–1612). Gerard's *Herball* is deservedly the most famous of the great fifteenth- and sixteenth-century garden and botanical works. His vast knowledge of plants is that of a true gardener as much as that of a learned botanist and apothecary to the king. His colorful turn of phrase, homely recommendations for medicinal and household uses of plants, and keen appreciation of the beauty of flowers make this book delightful and engrossing reading, even today. The woodcuts illustrating the work were those used in the 1590 botanical work *Eicones Plantarum* of Jacob Theador Tabernaemontanus; Gerard secured them from a Frankfurt printer.

Paradisi in Sole, Paradisus Terrestris (London, 1629) by John Parkinson (1567–1650). Heralding one of the best garden books of all time, Parkinson's title is a Latin pun on his own name, meaning "Park in Sun's Park on Earth." While the illustrations are naïve and crude, both aesthetically and in the information they give, his descriptions of growth habits and leaf and flower characteristics of plants are careful and precise.

Recipe Books

Because Mr. Huntington was interested in early printed books, the Library now contains a number of sixteenth- and seventeenth-century English recipe books. They bear little resemblance to modern cookbooks, with instructions written in narrative form and the measurements frequently vague (a "handful," a "few," or "a very good quantitie"). The books were usually not limited to recipes for preparing food but might also include instructions for killing lice, curing or preventing drunkenness, keeping venison from rotting, preserving a white complexion, or curing the plague as well as directions for making salves, oils, medicines, and cosmetics.

The first known recipe book to be printed in English appeared in 1500. Known as the *Boke of Cokery,* it was described as a "noble boke of festes [feasts] royalle and cookery, a boke for a pryncis [prince's] household or any other estates." Men wrote these early recipe books; women authors were rare. No woman's name appears as the author of any practical guidebook for housewives before 1640.

The Huntington cookbook holdings have grown over the years through the gifts of major collections. One is the Anne M. Cranston collection of 4,355 American cookbooks from the nineteenth and twentieth centuries and another is the extensive California cookbook collection formed by Philip S. and Helen Evans Brown, nationally recognized twentieth-century culinary experts. Included in the Brown collection is an extremely rare eighteen-page pamphlet by Hattie P. Bowman, *The Refugees' Cook Book, compiled by one of them, 50 recipes for 50 cents,* issued for victims of the 1906 San Francisco earthquake and fire.

A History of the Huntington Herb Garden

The herb garden is on the site of what was originally Mrs. Huntington's flower garden. Initially the area was planted with tulips, daffodils, narcissuses, and Spanish and Dutch irises. Later it changed from season to season, featuring both annuals and perennials, and eventually roses. Great quantities of these flowers filled vases in the house and on the loggia. Since Mrs. Huntington's eyesight was impaired and she could not appreciate a few flowers in a vase, massive displays were arranged. During the 1915 season, cut flowers sent to the home from the gardens and glasshouses for flower arrangements totaled 1,850 orchids (5 kinds), 3,900 pink and 3,000 white glasshouse roses, 2,800 outdoor roses, 3,300 red and 600 white glasshouse carnations, 600 cyclamens, 2,400 violets, 600 acacia branches, 1,300 daffodils, 1,000 narcissuses, 200 amaryllises, 2,200 branches of flowering shrubs, 1,000 lilies-of-the-valley, 3,500 irises, 1,800 sweet peas, 700 watsonias, 250 branches of heather, 250 stocks, 2,000 gladioluses, and 150 anthuriums.

Janet Wright, who wrote and lectured widely on herbs, converted this flower garden to an herb garden in the 1940s. When her husband died, Mrs. Wright moved to an apartment, leaving behind her beloved herb garden. When she became William Hertrich's secretary, she transplanted herbs from her home garden to a plot at the Huntington, and she tended the garden during her lunch hour for several years until joining a convent in 1956.

The garden lay neglected until 1975, when John MacGregor IV, a head gardener, became interested in restoring it. At that time almost all of the existing plants were removed and new brick paths replaced crumbling concrete ones. The design is reminiscent of open-knot gardens in late-Renaissance Europe and relates to the fine collection of sixteenth- and seventeenth-century herbals, garden books, cookbooks, housekeeping manuals, and other herb-related materials in the Huntington Library. Each bed was dedicated to herbs of a particular use, including medicines, cooking, salads, teas, confections, perfumes and cosmetics, sachets and insect repellents, and dyes.

In 1985 the garden was again refurbished, this time under the direction of Shirley Kerins, a licensed landscape architect and trained horticulturist, who became curator of the Huntington Herb Garden. At that time Kerins wished to make the garden look attractive and colorful, not an easy task when most herbs are plain and homely.

Map of the Huntington Herb Garden by Allison Mia Starcher

Under her direction, new herbs joined the Huntington Herb Garden. Research had uncovered herbal uses for several common garden plants, such as the English daisy, which was once called "bruisewort," qualifying it for a place in the medicinal bed. Johnny-jump-ups, known as "heart's ease," were considered both a remedy for heart ailments and an aphrodisiac, as Oberon knew in *A Midsummer Night's Dream.* The lovely columbine was also used medicinally, and the dwarf form creates a ribbon of color in two of the beds. This compact plant comes in shades of lavender, pink, mauve, claret, white, and old rose, all of which are in harmony with the alyssum or "madwort" growing nearby. A new bed was added for tussie mussies, bouquets of herbs and flowering plants used by Victorians to express their sentiments through the language of flowers. Many plants were labeled with interpretive signs, some with quotations from early herbals in the Huntington Library's rare book collection and others telling how the herbs were used in times past.

The Huntington Herb Garden Today

Today the Huntington Herb Garden is regarded as one of the finest in the country because of its extensive collection of herbs: native American plants, both well-known and obscure traditional English and European herbs, and herbs from Asia, Central America, and South America. Because of the mild Southern California climate, several semi-tropical herbs and spices such as ginger, galangal, lemon grass, and allspice are also in the garden.

A cadre of trained herb garden docents are stationed in the garden during public hours to answer questions or to explain the role of herbs in everyday life. Many people think of herbs only as seasonings for food, and others consider all herbs to be edible, a false and dangerous assumption. Alternative medicine devotees have been hailing herbs as the answer to specific health problems. We can buy herbal shampoos, herbal skin lotions, and herbal fragrances in stores. What is an herb and what is it for?

To a botanist, an herb or herbaceous plant is a plant with a non-woody stem. To an enthusiast, an herb is used for flavor, fragrance, medicine, cosmetics, dyes, or even symbolic messages. To a chef, an herb is a plant that comes from the temperate zones of the world, with leaves that can be used to flavor food. Spices, however, come from tropical areas and provide flavorful parts other than leaves. For example, cinnamon (bark), cloves (flower buds), ginger (roots, or more accurately rhizomes), and allspice (berries) are considered as spices.

The Huntington Herb Garden reflects all of these definitions of herbs. However, none of these definitions is complete. At the Huntington, we think of herbs as plants with domestic uses—plants that people grew or gathered from the wild to improve their lives.

Southern California's mild climate enables us to grow a wide range of plants; therefore, the Huntington includes flavoring plants such as ginger, turmeric, saffron, and allspice, which might be considered spices rather than herbs. But we ignore that hair-splitting definition—if a plant has a domestic use, we try to grow it, and this book celebrates all of the culinary useful plants growing in the Huntington Herb Garden.

A CELEBRATION OF HERBS

Plate 44

Hearts Eafe
Panfies
Eliz. Blackwell delin. sculp. et Pinx.

1 Flower
2 Flower cup
3 Seed Veffell
4 Seed

Viola tricola

CHAPTER 1

Learning to Use Herbs in Cooking

Becoming familiar with the flavors and intensity of herbs is essential to being able to use their full potential in cooking. Some are much stronger or more pungent than others, and fresh and dried versions of the same herb have different flavors. For example, fresh ginger root has a sharp, clean taste that does marvelous things for chicken and fish dishes. Powdered dried ginger, however, is quite mellow and lacks the zip of fresh ginger but works well in cookies and other baked goods.

Fresh tarragon has a sharp bite, hence its scientific name *Artemesia dracunculus* 'Sativa,' *dracunculus* meaning "little dragon." Dried tarragon is quite tame and sweeter. Cilantro, parsley, and chives are best fresh. Home-dried, they taste like dead grass; commercially dried, they are a little more flavorful.

Rosemary, thyme, and sweet marjoram taste the same fresh or dried. Because their leaves shrink in the drying process, you can expect the dried version to be slightly stronger than the fresh version.

Once you learn the flavors of various fresh and dried herbs, you can improvise; after all, that's part of the fun of cooking.

The Eight-Step Program for Learning to Cook with Herbs

Step One: Sample single-herb butters. To ½ cup (¼ pound) room-temperature butter or margarine, add 2 to 3 tablespoons of a minced fresh herb or 1 to 2 teaspoons of a dried herb. Store this mixture in a covered container in the refrigerator. Label each container according to the herb used.

Spread a little of the herb butter on a plain cracker, then taste and put the flavors in your memory. When you've learned the flavor of one herb, move on to the next until you've built up a memory bank of flavors. These dozen popular herbs make a good starter course:

BASIL ❧ CHIVES ❧ CILANTRO ❧ DILL
FENNEL ❧ MARJORAM ❧ MINT ❧ OREGANO
PARSLEY ❧ ROSEMARY ❧ SAGE ❧ TARRAGON

Consider the following uses for herb butters:

1 Spread on a cracker or use for canapés, hors d'oeuvres, or tea sandwiches. For example, dill butter spread on thin slices of bread and topped with sliced cucumbers, cooked shrimp, and a sprig of dill weed makes a lovely sandwich.
2 Place a dollop on hot cooked vegetables.
3 Press soft herb butter into a fancifully shaped plastic or rubber candy mold. Enclose in a zippered plastic bag and chill or freeze. When ready to use, press out the molded forms onto a serving plate. Or, shave into curls, chill, and serve with bread.
4 Place a dollop on hot grilled chicken, fish, or steak.
5 Add to the butter or oil used when sautéing chicken or fish.
6 Use to make a roux for sauces or gravies.

Don't be afraid to get creative. Use combination butters as you do the single butters, and combine the herbs in pairs, such as dill with chives or tarragon with garlic. Keep notes on what you've done so that you can repeat it (or learn from a disaster).

Step Two: Now that you can distinguish herbs such as fennel and dill, which look alike but don't taste the same, you're ready to move on. Next, try vegetable dips, flavoring them with the same herbs and using yogurt, sour cream, or cream cheese, singly or in combination. Garlic added to any of these dips enhances its character.

Step Three: Create mayonnaise sauces. To 1 cup of mayonnaise, add as much as ¼ to ⅓ cup snipped fresh dill. A tablespoon or 2 of both mint and chives along with the dill makes a pleasing sauce for fish. Or, for slices of tomatoes, add ⅓ cup minced basil, 3 tablespoons Parmesan cheese, and a clove of garlic, pressed, to 1 cup mayonnaise.

❧ PARTY IDEA ❧

Set out several herb butters surrounded by bread or crackers, and see if your guests can guess which herbs are in each one. If you wish to give hints, you might garnish the serving dish with a sprig of the herb. Or you might give a clue to the herb from some of the historic or horticultural anecdotes mentioned in this book, such as "This herb was found in King Tut's tomb."

Step Four: Try herb vinegars (see Chapter 4).

Step Five: Experiment with salad dressings and marinades. To make a vinaigrette or marinade, use various kinds of vinegars and oils in a formula of three parts oil to one part herb vinegar. For each cup of marinade, mix in ¼ cup fresh minced herbs or 2 to 3 tablespoons dried herbs. Use a 6-inch branch of rosemary or thyme to brush the marinade onto the meat or vegetables while grilling.

For mayonnaise-based dressings, use purchased, prepared mayonnaise for food-safety reasons. For each cup of mayonnaise, add ¼ to ⅓ cup fresh minced herbs or 1 to 2 tablespoons dried herbs, depending upon the strength of their flavor.

Step Six: Add fresh herbs to salads. Torn or shredded basil is a great way to start, but don't limit yourself to common sweet basil—try lemon basil, cinnamon basil, anise basil, or any of the other fifteen or more kinds of basil. You may have to grow some of these yourself. Follow the same timetable for seed and planting as you would for tomatoes in your area; they have similar needs and are happy companions in the garden or on the table.

Consider the many salad herbs, such as radicchio and arugula, discussed in the salad section. Don't forget the lovely edible flowers such as borage, daylilies, nasturtiums, chives, and garlic chive blossoms—they add delight and flavor to any salad.

Step Seven: Vary your favorite bread recipe by adding any of the seed herbs such as fennel, dill, caraway, poppy, nigella, or anise. Rosemary and chives also work well in breads. If you don't make your own bread, you can spread herb butters, with or without pressed garlic, onto purchased French or Italian breads, then heat or toast the breads lightly in the oven.

Step Eight: By now, you'll be experienced enough to experiment with all kinds of soups, stews, chowders, and sauces. Add fresh chives, garlic chives, parsley, cilantro, burnet, or chervil at the last minute, just before serving. The stronger flavored herbs are added early or midway through the cooking. One of these, the bay leaf, you should pull out of the jar and stick in your lapel: you've earned it! Bay laurel, or *Laurus nobilis,* is the ancient Greek and Roman emblem of success and reward.

Keeping Herbs in Balance

When cooking with herbs, remember to use a light hand in seasoning because herbs should enhance the food in a subtle way. If your guests remark that the dish you prepared tastes wonderful and ask which herbs you used, you have succeeded. However, sometimes you may want the herb flavor to be more pronounced, particularly if the name of the herb is found in the name of the dish. Anise-caraway bread, tarragon-marinated mushrooms, or rosemary potatoes would be disappointing if you could not taste the herbs that define them.

Generally, do not serve all highly seasoned dishes on a single occasion since the flavors will battle one another. As in drama or music, one or two pronounced themes are best offset with subtle counterpoints that balance the whole.

Mincing Fresh Herbs

Mincing large-leafed fresh herbs such as basil, sage, or sorrel is made easier by first stacking them horizontally. With scissors or a sharp knife, make three or four lengthwise cuts almost to the stem end. While still holding the leaves, cut crosswise into very fine dice. To make the basil "shreds" called for in some of the recipes, omit the lengthwise cuts and simply cut crosswise after stacking.

When mincing chives, cut the cluster of long blades into three-inch lengths. Now you have a much fatter, but shorter, clump to snip all at once right into your measuring spoon or cup.

The crescent-shaped blade of a mezzaluna is another tool for mincing fresh herbs quickly. It works on any cutting board, or you can buy one with its own matching bowl-shaped board. For the high-tech cook, a small food processor will make quick work of preparing a cup or more of minced parsley or another fresh herb.

Herb Blends

BOUQUET GARNI

This French term usually refers to a small gathering of herb sprigs tied together with string for easy removal before serving. The bouquet flavors marinades, soups, stews, poached fish, and other cooked foods. Sometimes dried herbs are added and tied together in little cloth bags.

A bay leaf is almost always part of a bouquet garni, along with parsley, thyme, sweet marjoram, chervil, and savory. Basil, fennel, coriander seeds, or peppercorns can also be added. Fresh herbs might be enclosed in two celery stalks tied together. The bouquet should be added during the last 15 to 30 minutes of cooking.

FINES HERBES

Traditionally, fresh parsley, tarragon, chives, and chervil make up this blend. Fines herbes are more delicate than the bouquet garni or herbes de Provence. Sometimes fresh summer savory, marjoram, or salad burnet are welcome additions. Fines herbes are used in sauces, soups, and egg and cheese dishes, as well as marinades. The fresh herbs are minced and added to the cooked food just before serving. Add fines herbes to scrambled eggs to make a nice lunch on short notice.

GREMOLATA

Gremolata is a combination of parsley, garlic, and orange and/or lemon zest. Sauté briefly 2 tablespoons chopped parsley, 2 cloves garlic, minced, and the zest of 2 oranges or lemons, finely minced. Add at the last minute to soups, stews, vegetables, or braised meat dishes such as osso buco.

HERBES DE PROVENCE

Lavender—an herb not generally used in American cooking—makes this blend so distinctive. As with curry, the components of herbes de Provence and their proportions will vary from town to town, or from cook to cook. However, certain ingredients are constant, such as thyme, rosemary, savory, and, of course, lavender. Fennel and marjoram are sometimes included. Sage, mint, basil, or bay leaves are added less often, but by no means are they excluded entirely. Create your own blend by using the following proportions of dried herbs as a guide:

3 tablespoons thyme
3 tablespoons marjoram
2 tablespoons savory

2 tablespoons rosemary
1 tablespoon lavender buds
1 tablespoon fennel seed

To adjust the combination of herbs, stir 2 teaspoons of the mixture into ¼ cup (2 ounces) of softened butter. Let the butter absorb the flavors for several hours, then taste on plain bread or crackers and add more of any herb to correct or balance the flavor. Store the dried herbs in an airtight container.

A popular way to use this blend is to make a paste with the herbs, olive oil, and, if you wish, a little salt and pepper. Rub on leg of lamb or lamb chops, roast chicken or chicken parts before cooking. This blend can also be made into a marinade with olive oil, wine, and a crushed garlic clove or two. Simply place the chicken, lamb, or fish in the marinade in a zippered plastic bag and refrigerate for at least 1 hour, or as long as 8 hours, before grilling. Another way to use herbes de Provence is to combine ¼ cup of the herb blend with ½ cup dried bread crumbs. Sauté in 2 tablespoons melted butter or olive oil and sprinkle on cooked vegetables just before serving.

Herbes de Provence have a special affinity for tomatoes and bell peppers. Consider it a happy marriage of Old World herbs with New World vegetables. Ratatouille, broiled tomatoes, or a stew that includes tomatoes works well with this mélange of herbs.

PERSILLADE

This mixture containing minced flat-leaf parsley and minced garlic
(fresh or sautéed briefly in olive oil) is added to a dish just before serving.

2 tablespoons packed fresh parsley, stemmed
3 tablespoons olive oil
2 cloves garlic, minced

½ teaspoon grated lemon zest
¼ teaspoon salt

Combine the parsley with oil, garlic, lemon zest, and salt in a blender. Purée until smooth. Refrigerate in a covered jar until ready to use. Thin with a little lemon juice if you wish to make it more tart. Goes well with lamb or beef.

Other Herb Blends

DRIED HERBS WITH LEMON BLEND

Lemon zest adds zip to this recipe.

> ## ❧ LEMON MIMICS ❧
>
> *A lemon flavor or scent appears in many different and unrelated herbs. Besides lemon balm and lemon thyme, you can find lemon verbena, lemon grass, lemon savory, and lemon-scented geranium. The Huntington Herb Garden has one small bed devoted to these citrus mimics, which were important to cooks who did not have year-round access to fresh lemons.*

Zest from 2 large lemons
1 tablespoon dried thyme leaves
1 tablespoon dried savory
1 tablespoon dried marjoram
1 tablespoon dried sage leaves, crumbled
1 tablespoon dried basil leaves, crumbled

Remove the zest from the lemons and mince. (Save the rest of the lemons for use at another time.) Spread the zest in a shallow baking pan or dish and dry in a 300-degree oven for 6 to 10 minutes, stirring occasionally. Remove.

In a small bowl, combine the herbs and lemon zest, mixing thoroughly. Store in an airtight container.

MAKES ABOUT 1/3 CUP

HERB BREAD CRUMB MIX

Sprinkle this mix on vegetables, pasta, or casseroles, or spread on chicken or fish as a coating before sautéing.

½ cup olive oil
4 cups dry bread crumbs
1 tablespoon dried basil, crumbled

1 tablespoon dried parsley
1 tablespoon dried tarragon, crumbled
1 tablespoon dried marjoram, crumbled

Heat the oil in a skillet over medium heat. Add the bread crumbs and herbs, stirring over low heat until well blended and toasted. Cool. The mix can be stored in the refrigerator for 1 to 2 months.

MORE HERB MIXTURES

Although excellent when made with fresh herbs, all of these mixtures can also be made with dried herbs.
Store these dried herb mixtures in airtight containers in a cool, dark place until needed; or, wrap and use as gifts.

1 For ground beef mixtures: 1 tablespoon each summer savory, basil, sweet marjoram, thyme, parsley, and lovage or celery leaves.

2 For vegetables: 1 tablespoon each summer savory, sweet marjoram, chervil, and basil.

3 For pork dishes: 1 tablespoon each sage, basil, and summer savory.

4 For lamb and veal dishes: 1 tablespoon each sweet marjoram, summer savory, and rosemary.

5 For egg and chicken dishes: 1 tablespoon each summer savory, tarragon, chervil, basil, and chives.

6 For poultry stuffing: 1 tablespoon each summer savory, sweet marjoram, basil, thyme, parsley, and celery or lovage leaves; and 1 teaspoon each sage leaves, minced fine, and dried lemon zest. Or, 3 tablespoons sage; 1 tablespoon each lemon thyme, lovage, and parsley; and 2 tablespoons marjoram.

7 For vegetable cocktails (add to 1 pint of liquid): ½ teaspoon each sweet marjoram, basil, tarragon, thyme, summer savory; and 1 tablespoon chopped chives.

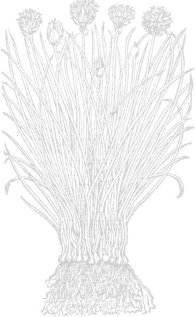

8 For fish (add to 2 cups of liquid): ¼ teaspoon each sweet marjoram, thyme, basil, and sage, plus crushed seeds of fennel. Or, 1 tablespoon each basil and parsley; 1½ teaspoons dill, tarragon, or fennel; and 1 bay leaf.

9 For soups and stews (add to 2 quarts of liquid): 1 teaspoon each parsley or chervil, thyme or summer savory, basil, and sweet marjoram. Or, 1 tablespoon each savory and lovage, 2 tablespoons marjoram, and 1½ teaspoons rosemary.

10 For tomato sauce: 2 tablespoons basil, 1 tablespoon each marjoram and parsley, and 1½ teaspoons oregano.

11 For salad herbs: 1 tablespoon each basil, parsley, and tarragon; and 1½ teaspoons thyme.

Plate 104.

Basil

Eliz. Blackwell delin. sculp. et Pinx.

1. *Flower*
2. *Fruit*
3. *Seed*

Basilicon or Ocimum.

Herb Butters, Sauces, Pestos, Salsas, and Marinades

Sauces with herbs are quick and easy to prepare and, for the most part, not expensive.

Today, sauce is no longer defined as previously in French cuisine—liquid thickened with a roux of fat and starch or eggs through slow cooking. Many sauces such as reductions, vegetable or fruit purées, coulis, and salsas contain little or no fat. Frequently, they are brightly flavored and a favorite of those watching their waistlines.

While we think of sauce as accompanying food, we all have encountered a sauce that was so delicious only the greatest self-control kept us from sneaking away and eating it with a spoon!

Herb Butters

Generally speaking, you can mix the herbs directly into softened butter. If you wish to pour the herb butter over food, heat the butter in a pan on the stove, in a warmed oven, or in the microwave just until melted. Then stir in the minced herbs.

AVOCADO BUTTER

Warning: this butter is addictive. Spoon onto cooled fish, or add a dollop to a bowl of tortilla soup.

½ cup (¼ pound) unsalted butter,
   at room temperature
½ cup ripe avocado, mashed with a fork
2 cloves garlic, minced

1 tablespoon lime juice
⅓ cup minced fresh flat-leaf parsley
Salt to taste

In a blender or food processor, whip the butter until soft and creamy. Blend in the avocado and garlic. Mix in the lime juice, parsley, and salt with a spoon. Serve at room temperature.

MAKES ABOUT 1 CUP

LEMON DILL BUTTER

Excellent with any fish or boiled potatoes.

½ cup (¼ pound) unsalted butter,
   at room temperature
4 teaspoons minced fresh shallots

4 teaspoons lemon juice
1 tablespoon minced fresh dill

In a bowl, mix the butter, shallots, lemon juice, and dill. Refrigerate in a covered container for several hours, overnight, or until ready to serve. Bring to room temperature before serving. Butter can be refrigerated up to 1 week.

MAKES ABOUT 1/2 CUP

TARRAGON GREEN PEPPERCORN BUTTER

A hearty butter that complements broiled steak or fish.

½ cup (¼ pound) unsalted butter, at room temperature
4 teaspoons brandy

1 tablespoon minced fresh tarragon
4 teaspoons green peppercorns
½ teaspoon soy sauce

In a bowl, mix the butter, brandy, tarragon, peppercorns, and soy sauce. Refrigerate in a covered container for several hours, overnight, or until ready to serve. Bring to room temperature before serving.

MAKES ABOUT 1/2 CUP

TOMATO ROSEMARY BUTTER

The tomato paste naturally tints the butter a pale salmon color.

½ cup (¼ pound) unsalted butter, at room temperature
1 tablespoon tomato paste

1 teaspoon lemon juice
1 teaspoon minced fresh rosemary
⅛ teaspoon white pepper

In a bowl, mix the butter, tomato paste, lemon juice, rosemary, and white pepper. Refrigerate in a covered container for several hours, overnight, or until ready to serve. Bring to room temperature before serving.

MAKES ABOUT 1/2 CUP

FAVORITE HERB BUTTER

Spread on hamburgers, sandwiches, steak, fish, green vegetables, or canapés, or use this butter when sautéing chicken or fish.

½ cup (¼ pound) butter, at room temperature
1 tablespoon minced fresh parsley
2 teaspoons minced fresh chives

1 tablespoon lemon juice
1 clove garlic, pressed
1 teaspoon crumbled dried tarragon

In a bowl, mix the butter, parsley, chives, lemon juice, garlic, and tarragon. Refrigerate in a covered container for several hours, overnight, or until ready to serve. Bring to room temperature before serving.

MAKES ABOUT 1/2 CUP

Mayonnaise, Yogurt, Cream, and Sour Cream Sauces

HERBED MAYONNAISE FOR SALMON

You can even make this with low-fat cottage cheese instead of mayonnaise; add the pine nuts later.
The sorrel adds its tart lemony flavor and is nice to use when lemons aren't available.

¼ cup fresh basil or sorrel

1½ cups mayonnaise

2 tablespoons chopped pine nuts

2 cloves garlic, minced

Blanch the basil or sorrel quickly in boiling water, drain, and pat dry. Mince the basil; add the mayonnaise, pine nuts, and garlic.

MAKES 1 1/2 CUPS

DILL MINT MAYONNAISE

For a refreshing summer appetizer, spoon a half teaspoon of this mayonnaise on sliced cucumbers or garden fresh tomatoes.

1 cup mayonnaise

⅓ cup minced fresh dill

1 to 2 tablespoons minced fresh mint

Mix the mayonnaise, dill, and mint in a bowl. Refrigerate in a covered glass container until ready to serve. Mayonnaise can be refrigerated for up to 1 week.

MAKES 1 GENEROUS CUP

HERBED MAYONNAISE SUBSTITUTE

Especially appealing for those who are dieting.

Mix low-fat cottage cheese with a combination of minced fresh herbs. Spread on sandwiches instead of mayonnaise.

CUCUMBER DILL SAUCE (RAITA)

This sauce complements spicy curry dishes and "cools" the tongue.

1 large cucumber, peeled, seeded, grated,
   and squeezed dry
1 cup low-fat plain yogurt
¼ cup minced fresh dill, or 3 teaspoons dried

½ teaspoon salt
Freshly ground pepper to taste
Dill sprigs for garnish

Combine the cucumber, yogurt, dill, salt, and pepper in a medium bowl. Cover and chill for at least 1 hour or up to 24 hours. Garnish with dill sprigs.

MAKES 1 2/3 CUPS

YOGURT SAUCE AUX FINES HERBES

Be sure to use fresh chervil, which has a lovely, delicate flavor. Serve grilled fish on a pool of this sauce.

1 teaspoon minced fresh tarragon,
   or ¼ teaspoon dried
½ teaspoon minced fresh thyme,
   or ¼ teaspoon dried
½ tablespoon minced fresh parsley,
   or ¼ teaspoon dried
2 teaspoons minced fresh chervil
½ tablespoon minced fresh chives
1 cup plain yogurt
1 teaspoon lemon juice
⅛ teaspoon ground white pepper
2 teaspoons Dijon mustard

Mix the tarragon, thyme, parsley, chervil, and chives with the yogurt, lemon juice, and white pepper. Add the mustard and stir until completely blended. Chill thoroughly before using. Adjust the lemon juice and seasonings before serving.

MAKES 1 1/2 CUPS

CHERVIL

The roots are likewise most excellent in a sallad, if they be boiled and afterwards dressed as the cunning Cooke knoweth how better than my selfe: notwithstanding I use to eat them with oile and vineger, being first boiled; which is very good for old people that are dull and without courage; it rejoiceth and comforteth the heart, and increaseth their lust and strength.

GERARD

Plate 415

Horse=radish.

Eliz. Blackwell delin. sculp. et Pinx.

} 1. *Flower* {

Raphanus sylvestris.

HORSERADISH YOGURT SAUCE

Serve with fish or spread on roast beef sandwiches.

½ cup plain yogurt

½ cup mayonnaise

2 to 3 tablespoons grated horseradish

1 to 1½ tablespoons lemon juice

Put the yogurt in a bowl and beat until smooth. Add the mayonnaise and mix. Add horseradish to taste, then stir in the lemon juice. The sauce should have a sharp flavor.

MAKES 1 CUP

HORSERADISH AND APPLE SAUCE

This Scandinavian sauce is traditionally served with hot or cold roast duck or goose. Try it with roast pork.

½ pound cooking apples, peeled, cored, and thickly sliced

3 tablespoons water

½ cup sour cream

3 to 4 tablespoons grated horseradish

Put the apples in a saucepan with the water. Cover and cook over low heat, stirring occasionally, until soft. Pass the apples through a food mill; set aside to cool. Stir in the sour cream, plus horseradish to taste. Best served at room temperature.

MAKES ABOUT 1 CUP

SPINACH SAUCE FOR COLD SALMON

Jaded palates will find this combination delicious.

2 quarts water

1 bunch spinach leaves

½ cup watercress, packed

10 sprigs fresh parsley

1 teaspoon dried English lavender flowers

1 cup mayonnaise

1 cup sour cream

1 teaspoon cream-style horseradish (optional)

2 tablespoons lemon juice

1 tablespoon minced fresh parsley

Bring the water to a boil. Add the spinach, watercress, parsley, and lavender; simmer 5 minutes. Remove from heat, drain, cool, and press out all of the excess water.

Combine the mayonnaise, sour cream, horseradish, and lemon juice; add to the spinach mixture. Stir in the minced parsley. Cover and refrigerate until ready to serve. Can be made earlier in the day.

MAKES ABOUT 3 CUPS

Oil-Based Sauces

MUSTARD DILL SAUCE

Add to grilled salmon fillets or smoked salmon.

⅓ cup Dijon or Pommery mustard
¼ cup sugar
2 tablespoons white vinegar

2 teaspoons powdered mustard
⅔ cup vegetable oil
½ cup minced fresh dill

Whisk together the mustard, sugar, vinegar, and powdered mustard in a bowl. Gradually add the oil while whisking until the mixture is the consistency of mayonnaise. Add the dill and mix well. Refrigerate in a covered container until ready to use. MAKES 1 CUP

SUMMER HERB SAUCE

Try with garden fresh tomatoes, barbecued chicken, toasted French bread, or your favorite pasta.

3 cups fresh parsley
1 cup mixed fresh herb leaves such as basil,
   fennel, marjoram, cilantro, or thyme
2 tablespoons Dijon mustard

2 cloves garlic, minced
⅓ to ½ cup olive oil
½ cup Parmesan cheese

In a blender or food processor, blend the parsley, herbs, mustard, garlic, olive oil, and Parmesan cheese until smooth. If the mixture is too thick, add more olive oil, 1 teaspoon at a time. Cover and chill. Freezes nicely.

MAKES ABOUT 1 1/2 CUPS

Cooked Sauces

The yearning for exquisitely seasoned, classic sauces will never end.

PARSLEY SAUCE

Parsley gives this sauce for beef, chicken, or fish a fresh but not overwhelming flavor.

2 tablespoons butter
1½ tablespoons all-purpose flour
1 cup hot chicken broth
¼ cup cream

Salt to taste
Freshly ground black pepper to taste
¼ cup chopped fresh flat-leaf parsley

Melt the butter in a small saucepan; stir in the flour. Cook for 1 minute, stirring. Remove from heat and gradually stir in the broth. Return to heat and bring to a boil, stirring. Lower the heat and simmer 3 minutes, stirring occasionally.

Stir in the cream and season to taste with salt and pepper. Just before serving, stir in the parsley. Serve hot.

MAKES 1 GENEROUS CUP

SORREL SAUCE

Serve this lovely green sauce hot, with pork chops or swordfish.

1 pound sorrel
1 tablespoon butter
1 tablespoon all-purpose flour

½ cup milk
1 teaspoon salt
2 tablespoons sugar, or to taste

Remove any rough stems from the sorrel; coarsely chop the leaves and set aside. Melt the butter in a large saucepan. Blend in the flour until smooth. Cook for 1 minute, stirring. Add the chopped sorrel. Cook over medium heat, stirring, until the leaves wilt and turn brownish-green, about 2 minutes. Stir in the milk. Bring to a boil and stir until the sauce thickens, about 3 minutes. Add the salt and sugar.

VARIATION: *Spinach also works well as a substitute for the sorrel.*

MAKES 1 CUP

FRESH HERB STEAK SAUCE

This piquant sauce will dress up your favorite grilled or pan-fried steak.

1 tablespoon oil
4 plum tomatoes, diced
⅓ cup pine nuts, toasted
2 tablespoons capers, drained
1 tablespoon chopped shallot
6 cloves garlic, minced
1 teaspoon minced fresh rosemary

1 teaspoon minced fresh thyme
1 teaspoon minced fresh oregano
1 teaspoon minced fresh tarragon
1 tablespoon Pernod
1 tablespoon dry white wine
1 tablespoon lemon juice
3 tablespoons butter, cut into pieces

Heat the oil in a large skillet. Add the tomatoes, pine nuts, capers, shallot, garlic, rosemary, thyme, oregano, and tarragon; cook for 2 minutes. Add the Pernod, wine, and lemon juice; simmer until reduced to a thick sauce. Whisk in the butter and pour over steak.

MAKES ABOUT 1 CUP

MINT SAUCE

Always welcome, this classic sauce is perfect with roast lamb.

1 ½ cups sugar
1 ½ cups cider vinegar
½ cup minced fresh mint leaves

Combine the sugar and vinegar in a medium saucepan. Bring to a boil; reduce heat and simmer uncovered for 20 minutes. Cool for 10 minutes. Stir in the mint leaves. Can be used immediately or stored in the refrigerator in a covered container.

MAKES 1 1/2 CUPS

ROSEMARY MINT SAUCE

Especially good with lamb or pork, rosemary adds a robust flavor to this mint sauce variation.

2 cups fresh mint leaves
1 cup dry white wine
½ cup white wine vinegar

½ cup water
¼ cup sugar
¼ cup minced fresh rosemary

Combine the mint, wine, vinegar, and water in a blender. Pour the mixture into a small saucepan and stir in the sugar. Bring to a boil and simmer over medium heat until the liquid is reduced by half and syrupy. Add the rosemary and simmer 1 minute, until slightly thickened.

MAKES A GENEROUS 1/3 CUP

BLENDER BÉARNAISE SAUCE

You can quickly make this old favorite with many uses. Wonderful as a dip for artichoke leaves or served with fresh cooked asparagus, this sauce also can be stored in a covered container and refrigerated for up to a week.

3 egg yolks
1 tablespoon lemon juice
¼ teaspoon salt
Pinch of white pepper
1 teaspoon minced fresh onion

1 teaspoon minced fresh parsley
½ teaspoon dried tarragon
½ cup (¼ pound) butter,
  melted and still hot

Place the egg yolks, lemon juice, salt, white pepper, onion, parsley, and tarragon in a blender. Blend for 2 seconds. Remove the cover and gradually drip in the melted butter while blending. The sauce will thicken immediately. Serve with meat or vegetables.

MAKES 3/4 CUP

Pestos

The word *pesto* comes from the use of a mortar and pestle, which in Italy are used to grind fresh basil into a paste along with garlic, pine nuts, Parmesan cheese, and olive oil. Today, the word refers to any sauce made from a base of ground fresh herbs, with the possible addition of nuts, cheese, and olive oil. This section includes rosemary pesto, cilantro pesto, and even arugula pesto, not to mention several variations on basil pesto. All deliver that intense jolt of flavor we have come to appreciate.

Enjoy pestos on pastas and pizzas, in soups or stews, on grilled meats and hamburgers, or mix them with soft cheeses as a dip or spread for crostini.

TRADITIONAL PESTO

Aromatic and pungent!

¾ cup pine nuts, toasted

2 cups packed fresh basil, stemmed

½ teaspoon salt

⅛ teaspoon pepper

½ cup (4 ounces) grated Parmesan cheese

½ cup (4 ounces) grated Romano cheese

2 cloves garlic, peeled and quartered

½ cup olive oil

In a blender or food processor, mix the pine nuts, basil, salt, pepper, Parmesan cheese, Romano cheese, and garlic at high speed, just until smooth. Gradually pour in the oil, processing until smooth. Serve immediately, or cover and refrigerate for up to 5 days. Can be frozen for up to 6 months (but omit cheese).

🌿 VARIATION: *Substitute 2 cups fresh spinach leaves and 2 teaspoons crumbled dried leaf basil for the fresh basil. Or, substitute 1 ¾ cups finely snipped fresh parsley (no stems) and 2 tablespoons crumbled dried leaf basil for the fresh basil.*

MAKES 1 1/3 CUPS

PURPLE BASIL PESTO

Don't be alarmed at the color. Purple basil has a nice fruity taste that works well with chicken or fish.

2 cups fresh purple basil

¼ cup pine nuts or walnuts, toasted

2 or 3 cloves garlic

3 tablespoons lemon juice

Pinch of salt

½ cup olive oil

¼ cup freshly grated
Parmesan cheese

Combine the basil, pine nuts or walnuts, garlic, lemon juice, salt, and olive oil in a food processor or blender. Stir in the Parmesan cheese.　　MAKES ABOUT 1 CUP

ARUGULA PESTO

Try this sauce with chicken sandwiches, or on pasta with cooked chicken and peas.

2 bunches arugula
1 clove garlic
3 tablespoons pine nuts, toasted
½ cup extra-virgin olive oil

Pinch of cayenne
Ground pepper to taste
½ cup (4 ounces) grated Parmesan cheese

Stem and chop the arugula (makes 2 cups packed). In a food processor, blend the arugula, garlic, pine nuts, olive oil, cayenne, and ground pepper until the mixture resembles a coarse paste. Add the Parmesan cheese and mix well.

MAKES A SCANT 1 CUP

MINT PESTO

Adds a finishing touch to any ground lamb loaf or patties.

3 cloves garlic, minced
2 tablespoons olive oil
1 tablespoon sugar

1 cup minced fresh mint leaves
½ cup pine nuts, finely chopped

Cook the garlic in olive oil in a large skillet until transparent, about 2 minutes. Remove from heat and stir in the sugar until dissolved. Set aside to cool completely. Add the mint and pine nuts; stir to combine. Refrigerate in a covered container until ready to use.

MAKES ABOUT 1 CUP

PESTO CUBES

Conveniently stored in the freezer, these cubes provide a concentrated burst of herb flavor for soups and sauces.

4 cloves garlic
2 cups fresh basil

1 teaspoon salt
½ cup olive oil

Place the garlic in a food processor or blender and process until very finely minced. Add the basil and salt. Add the oil gradually to bind the basil. Spoon into ice cube trays and freeze. When the cubes are frozen, remove them and store in plastic bags in the freezer.

MAKES 6 CUBES, ABOUT 3 OUNCES EACH

GARLIC LOVERS' PESTO

Do NOT attend the theater after enjoying this pesto. However, for a nice after-the-theater snack, simply spread on grilled polenta or toasted French bread rounds, topped with shrimp.

2 tablespoons pine nuts, toasted
2 cups packed fresh basil
6 cloves garlic
½ teaspoon salt

¾ cup virgin olive oil
⅔ cup freshly grated Romano
    and/or Parmesan cheese

Purée the pine nuts, basil, garlic, and salt in a blender or food processor. With the machine running, add the olive oil and process until well blended. Add the cheese; pulse to combine. Refrigerate in a covered glass jar.

MAKES 2 CUPS

OIL-FREE PESTO

Vegetable broth or mineral water reduces the amount of fat in this pesto.

8 cloves garlic
3 cups loosely packed chopped fresh basil
2 cups chopped fresh spinach leaves
¼ cup pine nuts
¼ cup (2 ounces) finely grated Parmesan cheese

1 teaspoon lemon juice
¼ teaspoon freshly ground black pepper
2 to 4 tablespoons mineral water
    or vegetable broth

Combine the garlic, basil, spinach, pine nuts, Parmesan cheese, lemon juice, and pepper in a food processor or blender. Gradually add the water or broth while processing, making the pesto as thick or thin as desired.

MAKES 1 GENEROUS CUP

SPICY CILANTRO PESTO

Surprisingly delicious when tossed with fettuccine or served as a dip with raw vegetables or chips.

2½ cups fresh cilantro, stemmed
and coarsely chopped
½ cup (4 ounces) freshly grated
Parmesan cheese
½ cup pine nuts or walnuts
24 cloves garlic, chopped

¼ cup lime juice
1 tablespoon plus 1 teaspoon chili powder
1 tablespoon ground cumin
1 teaspoon dried crushed red pepper
1 teaspoon salt
¾ cup olive oil

Combine the cilantro, Parmesan cheese, pine nuts or walnuts, garlic, lime juice, chili powder, cumin, red pepper, and salt in a blender or food processor. With the machine running, gradually add the oil through the feed tube; blend until incorporated. Season with more pepper and salt, if desired. Can be refrigerated for up to 1 week, or frozen for up to 1 month.

MAKES 2 1/2 CUPS

ROSEMARY PESTO

Excellent with chicken, lamb, or boiled new potatoes.

2 cups lightly packed fresh parsley
1 cup lightly packed fresh rosemary
3 tablespoons pine nuts, toasted
2 cloves garlic, peeled

½ cup olive oil
2 tablespoons unsalted butter, melted
¼ cup Parmesan cheese
Salt and pepper to taste

In a blender or food processor, combine the parsley, rosemary, pine nuts, and garlic. Process into a fine paste, scraping down the sides of the bowl once or twice. With the machine running, pour the oil and butter through the feed tube in a slow, steady stream until the pesto is smooth and creamy. Pour mixture into a bowl and stir in the Parmesan cheese by hand; season with salt and pepper.

Transfer the pesto to a jar. Cover the surface with a film of olive oil. Seal the jar with a tight-fitting lid and refrigerate for up to 3 months. If you wish to freeze this pesto, prepare it without adding the cheese. Add the cheese after the pesto has thawed and is ready to serve.

MAKES ABOUT 1 CUP

MARIA BLUMBERG'S PAD THAI PESTO

Thai basil, dried shrimp powder, red chili with garlic paste, and fish sauce are available in Asian food markets. An overwhelming favorite when we "testoed" pestos.

1 bunch (approximately 1 cup lightly packed) fresh Thai basil
2 cloves garlic, crushed
1 tablespoon dried shrimp powder
2 teaspoons red chili with garlic paste, or to taste

3 tablespoons Thai fish sauce
1 tablespoon sugar
Juice of 1 lime
3 tablespoons peanuts, roasted
¼ tablespoon black pepper
¼ cup canola or peanut oil

Place basil, garlic, shrimp powder, red chili, fish sauce, sugar, lime juice, peanuts, pepper, and oil in a food processor. Pulse the processor a few times; then blend until mixture is relatively smooth. Use over any type of pasta or rice, as a stir fry sauce, or instead of the Pad Thai sauce with your Pad Thai recipe.

MAKES A SCANT 1 CUP

TARRAGON WALNUT PESTO

Serve this nutty pesto with fish, vegetables, pasta, or grilled chicken.

1 cup fresh tarragon
2 cloves garlic, peeled
½ teaspoon salt
1 tablespoon green peppercorns, drained

1 tablespoon lemon juice
1 cup walnut halves
½ cup olive oil
¼ cup warm water

In a blender or food processor, combine the tarragon, garlic, and salt. Process into a fine paste, scraping down the sides of the bowl once or twice. Add the peppercorns, lemon juice, and walnuts; process until smooth. With the machine running, pour the oil through the feed tube in a slow, steady stream until the pesto is smooth and creamy. If the pesto is too thick, add water through the feed tube, 1 teaspoon at a time, until the desired thickness is reached.

Transfer the pesto to a jar. Cover the surface with a film of olive oil. Seal the jar with a tight-fitting lid and refrigerate for up to 3 months, or freeze.

MAKES 1 GENEROUS CUP

Salsas

Thanks to food processors, salsas are quick and easy to prepare and require little or no cooking. They appeal to the diet-conscious because they contain little or no fat, and their robust, intense flavor is a nice contrast to the more delicately flavored traditional sauces.

SALSA FRESCA

Chilies vary greatly in terms of hotness but you can adjust the "heat" of a salsa by adding more or fewer chilies.

4 large tomatoes, peeled and finely chopped
1 cup minced onion
2 cloves garlic, minced
1 (4-ounce) can diced green chilies
1 jalapeño chili, seeded and minced

½ cup chopped fresh cilantro
1 tablespoon lemon juice
1 teaspoon salt
Freshly ground pepper to taste

Combine the tomatoes, onion, garlic, chilies, jalapeño, cilantro, lemon juice, salt, and pepper in a medium bowl. Store covered in the refrigerator, and remove from the refrigerator 30 minutes before serving. Can be made up to 3 days ahead.

MAKES ABOUT 2 GENEROUS CUPS

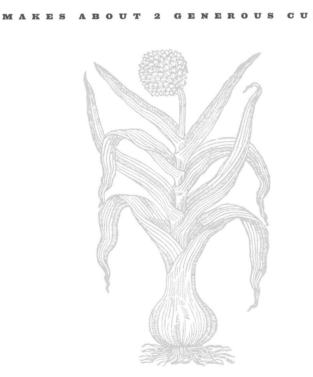

TOMATILLO SALSA

Try this light and spicy salsa with grilled meat or seafood, or serve with scrambled eggs inside warmed corn tortillas. Also good with enchiladas suizas made with flour tortillas. For the diet-conscious, this is an excellent topping for cottage cheese.

½ cup chicken broth
1 cup coarsely chopped onion
¾ pound fresh tomatillos,
    husked and quartered
1 jalapeño chili, seeded and minced
1 serrano chili, seeded and minced

2 cloves garlic, minced
¼ cup chopped fresh cilantro
½ teaspoon ground cumin
1 tablespoon lemon juice
¼ teaspoon salt

In a medium skillet, heat the chicken broth over medium heat. Add the onion and simmer, covered, for 5 minutes. Add the tomatillos and cook, covered, for 5 minutes.

Cool slightly and pour the onion-tomatillo mixture into a food processor. Process until coarsely chopped. Add jalapeño and serrano chilies, garlic, cilantro, cumin, lemon juice, and salt and process briefly until combined. Taste for seasoning.

Pour into a storage container and cool. Refrigerate, covered, until ready to use. Can be made up to 5 days ahead.

MAKES 2 CUPS

PAPAYA MINT SALSA

Surprising, and a refreshing accompaniment to grilled chicken or seafood.

2 large fresh tomatoes (1 pound), peeled,
    seeded, and chopped
1 ½ cups chopped fresh papaya
1 jalapeño chili, seeds removed, minced

½ cup minced red onion
½ cup finely chopped fresh mint leaves
2 tablespoons lime juice
½ teaspoon salt

Combine the tomatoes, papaya, jalapeño, red onion, mint, lime juice, and salt in a medium bowl. Cover and refrigerate until ready to serve. This salsa is best enjoyed the day it is made.

MAKES ABOUT 3 CUPS

MINT

Wormes, eat powder of Mints with milke.

Belly bound, eat Mints. Colour bad, use Mints daily.

Mints are healthfull at any time.

LANGHAM

ONION MINT RELISH

With a tart-sweet mint marinade, this relish pairs well with barbecued chicken, or add to green salad.

¼ cup rice vinegar, or white wine vinegar,
   mixed with 1 teaspoon sugar
2 teaspoons sugar
2 tablespoons minced fresh mint leaves

3 to 4 cups crisp raw onion shreds
½ cup shredded carrot
Salt to taste

   Mix the rice or white wine vinegar and sugar in a medium bowl until the sugar dissolves. Mix in the mint, onion shreds, and carrot; add salt. Serve, or cover and chill for up to 4 hours.

MAKES 3 TO 4 CUPS

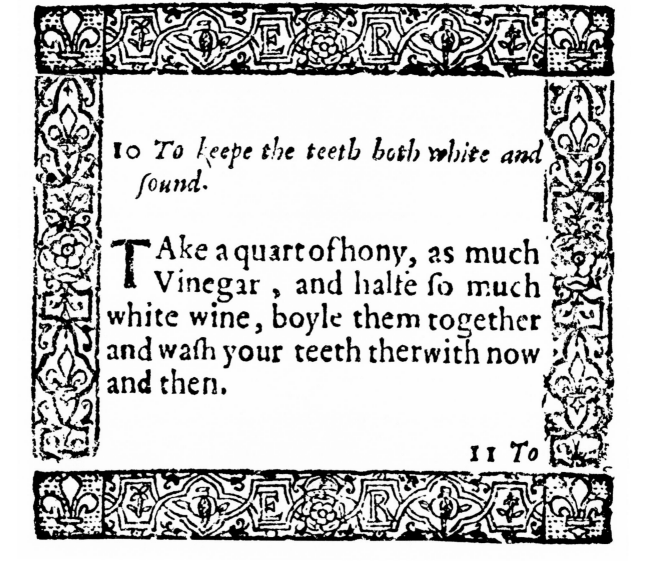

10 *To keepe the teeth both white and sound.*

TAke a quart of hony, as much Vinegar, and halfe so much white wine, boyle them together and wash your teeth therwith now and then.

11 *To*

To keepe the teeth both white and sound. Take a quart of hony, as much Vinegar, and halfe so much white wine, boyle them together and wash your teeth therewith now and then.

SIR HUGH PLATT, *Delightes for Ladies, to adorne their persons, tables, closets, and distillatories,* 1609 edition (first published about 1600).

Dentists were unknown in this period, and the self-sufficient household produced its own mouthwash—and soap. This particular recipe may have had additional medicinal qualities; heated, it would have been a good substitute for a hot toddy.

Marinades

For safety's sake, when using *any* marinade remember to boil it for 5 minutes after you've removed the meat, if you will be using it as a sauce or to baste the meat while it cooks. For each cup of marinade, mix in ¼ cup fresh minced herbs or 2 to 3 tablespoons dried herbs. You can also use a 6-inch branch of rosemary or thyme to brush the marinade onto the meat or vegetables while grilling.

UNCOOKED MARINADE WITH WINE

For this marinade, use white wine for chicken or fish, red wine for red meat.

1 cup wine

8 cloves

1 cup water

1 medium onion, chopped

6 peppercorns

1 clove garlic, crushed

1 bay leaf

2- or 3-inch sprig sweet marjoram

2- or 3-inch sprig lemon thyme

Combine the wine, cloves, water, onion, peppercorns, garlic, bay leaf, marjoram, and lemon thyme.

MAKES 2 CUPS OF MARINADE, ENOUGH FOR ABOUT 5 POUNDS OF MEAT OR POULTRY

ROSEMARY, LEMON, AND HONEY-MUSTARD MARINADE

Delicious with chicken, but also works well with lamb kebabs, beef, or pork.

½ cup lemon juice

3 tablespoons Dijon mustard

2 tablespoons honey

1 tablespoon minced fresh rosemary

1 pound boneless, skinless chicken breasts

Fresh rosemary sprigs for garnish

In a large zippered plastic bag, mix together the lemon juice, mustard, honey, and rosemary. Add the chicken and turn to coat. Squeeze out the excess air, close the bag, and chill for at least 30 minutes, or up to 1 day, turning occasionally to coat the chicken evenly with the marinade.

Remove the chicken and discard the remaining marinade. Grill the chicken and serve garnished with fresh rosemary sprigs.

SERVES 4

Plate 211.

Thyme.

Eliz. Blackwell delin. sculp. et Pinx.

1. *Flower.*
2. *Flower separate.*
3. *Calix.*
4. *Seed.*

Thymus.

CHAPTER 3

Appetizers

Fresh herbs can serve both as attractive, flavorful ingredients and as garnishes. For instance, putting a sprig of dill under a piece of shrimp or using chervil leaves to accompany an egg- or cheese-based canapé enriches both the taste and the eye appeal.

Herb flowers are even more intriguing. Here's a favorite that can be made on short notice: gather some blue borage flowers, yellow daylilies, and red nasturtium flowers from the garden; rinse and pat dry. Spread herb butter on round crisp crackers. Then place the whole borage flowers on one-third of the crackers, the round petals of nasturtiums on another third, and long daylily petals, snipped into squares, on the remaining crackers. The combination of three primary colors and three primary shapes will provide a visual and culinary treat perfect for any gathering.

HERB SAMPLER PLATE

See if your guests can name the herbs used in this appetizer.

1 pound fresh mozzarella

1 baguette, cut into ¼-inch slices
and lightly toasted

1 tablespoon each of assorted
fresh herbs, minced

Slice each piece of mozzarella into ¼-inch-thick disks. If the pieces are larger than 1¼ inches in diameter, cut in half. Place each portion on a toasted baguette slice. Sprinkle a pinch of minced herbs or herb seeds on top of the cheese.

Place the toasts on a bed of fresh lettuce or arugula. Garnish with red or yellow pear or cherry tomatoes. Or, use sprigs of various herbs to garnish the plate.

❧ NOTE: *Try any of the following: various basils, including purple, lemon, and cinnamon; rosemary; thyme; sage; parsley; cilantro, chives, and garlic chives; mint; sweet marjoram (particularly nice if you use the small knots or buds); caraway seed; anise seed; nigella seed; or borage, arugula, or nasturtium flowers.*

MAKES ABOUT 18 SLICES

TARRAGON SHRIMP

Tarragon is splendid with seafood.

3 cups medium shrimp, cooked,
peeled, and deveined

2 tablespoons minced shallots

1 tablespoon chopped fresh tarragon

Zest of 1 lemon, minced

2 tablespoons white wine vinegar

3 tablespoons sour cream,
regular or reduced fat

½ cup mayonnaise

Salt and pepper to taste

crostini or crackers

Roughly chop the shrimp into ½-inch pieces and put in a bowl. Add the shallots, tarragon, lemon zest, and vinegar; toss. In a separate bowl, mix the sour cream and mayonnaise. Fold into the shrimp mixture; season with salt and pepper. To serve, place in a bowl and surround with crostini.

❧ VARIATION: *You can substitute fresh dill leaves for the tarragon. Or, try 1 teaspoon fresh tarragon and 2 teaspoons fresh dill. Crème fraîche can also be substituted for the sour cream.*

SERVES 8 TO 12

SAUSAGE CHEESE SQUARES

A hearty fall or winter appetizer. Serve warm from the oven.

2 pounds Italian sausage, mild or hot
1 large onion, finely chopped
2 cloves garlic, minced
4 ounces mushrooms, sliced
1 tablespoon minced fresh basil, or ½ teaspoon dried
1 teaspoon minced fresh mint, or ½ teaspoon dried
1 teaspoon minced fresh oregano, or ½ teaspoon dried
¼ cup chopped fresh parsley
8 eggs, beaten
⅓ cup fine bread crumbs
4 cups shredded mozzarella cheese

BASIL

Basil also helps with Bitings venomous, Eye-ach and griefes, Flux of cold, Giddinesse, Heart Griefs, Head swimming, Masels, Melancholy, Warts, Windinesse, and Wormes . . .

LANGHAM

Preheat the oven to 325 degrees. Remove the casings from the sausages and crumble the meat into a large skillet. Stir over medium-high heat until browned. Set aside the cooked sausage. Drain the fat and discard all but 2 tablespoons. Add the onion, garlic, mushrooms, basil, mint, oregano, and parsley; stir until the vegetables and herbs are limp.

Stir in the eggs. Stir in the bread crumbs, mozzarella, and sausage.

Spread out evenly in a 10 × 15-inch baking dish. Bake for 30 to 35 minutes, until the mixture is firm in the center. Let cool slightly for handling, if serving as an appetizer.

Cut into 1-inch squares or diamonds to make 150 pieces. Or, serve hot as a luncheon entrée; cut into large rectangles.

MAKES 9 SERVINGS

NASTURTIUM APPETIZERS

Brightly colored and peppery-flavored flowers will get your guests' attention.
Use unsprayed flowers, fresh from the garden. Remove the hair-like stamens, pinching them
out with thumb and forefinger, to create more of a hollow in which to place the filling.

1 (8-ounce) package cream cheese,
   at room temperature
3 tablespoons sugar
3 tablespoons chopped walnuts

2 tablespoons grated orange zest
¼ teaspoon almond extract (optional)
36 fresh nasturtium flowers,
   rinsed and patted dry

Combine the cream cheese, sugar, walnuts, orange zest, and almond extract. Spoon the filling into a plastic bag. Cut off one small corner of the bag with scissors. Squeeze the bag to pipe the mixture into the center of each flower an hour or two before serving. Line the serving platter with nasturtium leaves and place the flowers on the leaves.

MAKES 36 APPETIZERS

SMOKED SALMON ROLLUPS

Make this pretty dish up to a day ahead of time and refrigerate until ready to slice and serve.

1 (8-ounce) package cream cheese,
   at room temperature
2 tablespoons sweet mustard
1 tablespoon sour cream
4 (9-inch) flour tortillas

12 ounces smoked salmon, thinly sliced
2 tablespoons minced fresh dill
2 tablespoons minced fresh chives
1 cup shredded lettuce
Fresh dill sprigs for garnish

DILL

In the Middle Ages and for centuries later, dill was thought to have magical powers. It was also thought to protect one from magic as well! Its English name is derived from the Norse word dilla, *meaning to lull. Dill water was given to colicky babies to help them expel gas.*

Combine the cream cheese, mustard, and sour cream. Spread the tortillas with the cheese mixture. Divide the salmon and arrange evenly on top. Leave a ½-inch border of cheese at the top of each tortilla so that it will stick to itself when rolled up. Sprinkle with dill, chives, and lettuce; roll up tightly, pressing to seal.

Wrap in plastic and refrigerate for at least 2 hours. To serve, unwrap and slice evenly, discarding the ends. Serve spiral side up, garnished with dill sprigs.

MAKES ABOUT 8 SLICES PER TORTILLA

HERB AND FETA CHEESE ROLLUPS

Have you noticed how pinwheel-shaped appetizers always disappear first?

Chicken

3 whole chicken breasts, boned,
    skinned, and halved
4 tablespoons butter or margarine, melted
Salt and pepper to taste

Filling

8 ounces feta cheese, crumbled
1 clove garlic, crushed

Coating

½ cup all-purpose flour
2 eggs, beaten
½ cup fine sourdough bread crumbs
¼ cup Parmesan cheese
1 teaspoon minced fresh parsley
1 teaspoon minced fresh thyme
1 teaspoon minced fresh rosemary

Sauce

¼ cup (2 ounces) butter or margarine
1 teaspoon minced fresh parsley
1 teaspoon minced fresh thyme
1 teaspoon minced fresh rosemary
½ cup dry white wine

❧ PARSLEY ❧

It is most pleasant unto the mouth and stomach.

Persely healeth fishes that are sick if it be casten

into them in the ponds, that they may eat it.

TURNER, 1562

Preheat the oven to 350 degrees. Lightly coat the bottom of a shallow baking dish with oil; set aside.

Flatten the chicken breasts between sheets of waxed paper. Brush melted butter on top of each chicken breast. Salt and pepper to taste.

Combine the feta cheese and garlic; spoon mixture onto the middle of each chicken breast, dividing evenly. Roll the breasts into loose cylinders.

Place the flour on waxed paper. Dredge the chicken rolls in flour. Beat the eggs in a small bowl. Dip the chicken rolls in beaten egg, allowing the excess to drain. Combine the bread crumbs, Parmesan cheese, and 1 teaspoon each of the parsley, thyme, and rosemary. Dredge the rolls in the bread crumb mixture. Arrange the chicken rolls, seam side down, in the baking dish.

To make the sauce, melt the butter in a small skillet; remove from heat and stir in parsley, thyme, and rosemary. Pour the sauce evenly over the chicken. Bake uncovered for 30 minutes. Add the wine and bake for another 20 minutes.

Place the chicken rolls on a platter. Scrape down and stir the sauce; pour it around the chicken, or serve separately.

MAKES 6 SERVINGS

Plate 417.

Caper.

1. Flower.
2. Fruit.
3. Fruit open.
4. Calix.
5. Seed.

Capparis.

Eliz. Blackwell delin. Sculp. et Pinx.

TOMATO, CHEESE, AND HERB TART

An easy recipe that shows off fresh herbs.

5 medium tomatoes, cut into ½-inch-thick slices

½ package (8 ounces) frozen puff pastry, thawed

4 ounces mozzarella cheese, grated

4 ounces aged provolone cheese, grated

Salt and freshly ground pepper to taste

¼ cup freshly grated Parmesan cheese

1 tablespoon olive oil

1 tablespoon minced fresh thyme

1 tablespoon minced fresh chives

1 teaspoon minced fresh oregano

Preheat the oven to 375 degrees. Cut each tomato slice in half. Place the tomato slices on paper towels and let drain for 30 to 45 minutes.

Brush a baking sheet with olive oil. On a lightly floured surface, roll out the puff pastry sheet into a 14 × 12-inch rectangle. Crimp the edges of the pastry, making the sides ½ inch tall. Transfer to a baking sheet and prick the crust all over with a fork.

Bake for 15 minutes, until golden, piercing with a fork every 5 minutes to deflate, if necessary. Sprinkle crust with mozzarella cheese and provolone cheese and set aside. (This can be prepared 4 hours ahead, and left to stand at room temperature.)

Increase the oven temperature to 425 degrees. Arrange the tomatoes on the crust in slightly overlapping rows, completely covering the pastry. Season to taste with salt and pepper. Sprinkle Parmesan cheese, olive oil, thyme, chives, and oregano over the tart.

Bake for about 10 minutes, until the tomatoes are heated through and the cheese melts. Cut into 1½- to 2-inch squares for passed appetizers, or into large squares to serve as a first course.

VARIATION: *Italian fontina, Romano, or pecorino cheese can be substituted for the provolone.*

MAKES 6 TO 8 SERVINGS

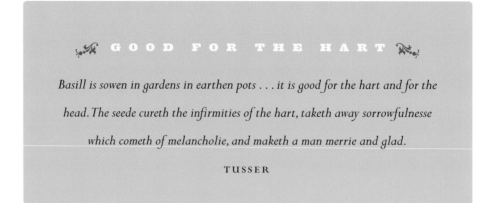

✦ GOOD FOR THE HART ✦

Basill is sowen in gardens in earthen pots . . . it is good for the hart and for the head. The seede cureth the infirmities of the hart, taketh away sorrowfulnesse which cometh of melancholie, and maketh a man merrie and glad.

TUSSER

HERBED MINI-MEATBALLS

This popular and hearty appetizer can be made in quantity ahead of time. Simply reheat before serving.

8 ounces mushrooms, sliced

4 tablespoons butter or margarine

1 medium onion, chopped

2 pounds ground turkey or lean ground beef

1 teaspoon salt, or to taste

¼ teaspoon freshly ground pepper

2 teaspoons minced fresh tarragon,
    or ½ teaspoon dried tarragon, crumbled

3 to 4 fresh basil leaves, minced

2 tablespoons flour

⅓ cup tomato paste

1 (10-ounce) can beef consommé

2 tablespoons Worcestershire sauce

1 tablespoon vinegar

1 cup sour cream or yogurt (optional)

Sauté the mushrooms in a large skillet using 2 tablespoons of the butter. Remove and set aside. Add the remaining 2 tablespoons butter and cook the onion until golden; remove and set aside with the mushrooms. Shape the ground turkey or beef into bite-sized balls. Brown, draining off any fat if necessary. Sprinkle the meatballs with the salt, pepper, tarragon, basil, and flour. Add the tomato paste, consommé, Worcestershire sauce, and vinegar. Cover and simmer 10 minutes. Add the mushrooms and onion. Remove from heat and stir in the sour cream or yogurt, if desired. Heat through, but do not allow to boil.

This can be made ahead, covered and refrigerated, until ready to heat and serve. It can be frozen without the sour cream or yogurt, adding this later, when heating to serve.

MAKES 6 TO 8 SERVINGS

BASIL-PROSCIUTTO-WRAPPED SHRIMP

Prepare skewers ahead of time and refrigerate until ready to grill.

Dipping Sauce

1 clove garlic
⅓ cup red wine vinegar
Salt and pepper to taste
2 tablespoons Dijon mustard
⅔ cup light olive oil

Skewers

24 fresh basil leaves, stemmed
24 extra-large raw shrimp, peeled and deveined
4 ounces prosciutto, thinly sliced and trimmed of fat
24 short wooden skewers, soaked in water

Place the garlic in a blender or food processor; process until minced. Add the vinegar, salt, pepper, and mustard. With the machine running, gradually add the olive oil. Place in a serving dish and set aside.

Wrap a basil leaf around each shrimp, then wrap a slice of prosciutto around the basil leaf. Thread each shrimp onto the end of a skewer, securing the prosciutto. Heat the grill or broiler. Grill the skewered shrimp approximately 4 inches from the heat source for 5 minutes, turning 3 to 4 times to cook evenly. The shrimp will turn pink when done. Be careful not to overcook.

Serve immediately with the dipping sauce.

MAKES 8 SERVINGS

GOOD FOR THE STOMACKE

Plinie *writeth that the same [basil] eaten is very good and convenient for the stomacke, and that if be drunken with Vineger it dryeth away ventosities or windiness, stayeth the appetite or desire to vomit, provoketh urine, besides this he saith, it is good for the hydropsie, and for them that hath the Jaunders.* DODOENS

NIGELLA-CHEESE-STUFFED PHYLLO TRIANGLES

The lovely, haunting flavor of ancient nigella seeds comes through in these tasty morsels. If you can find Armenian string cheese made with nigella seeds, use that. Otherwise, use whatever mozzarella or string cheese is available.

1 package frozen phyllo dough
1 cup ricotta cheese
2 cups shredded mozzarella or string cheese
2 teaspoons nigella seeds
1 tablespoon minced fresh parsley

1 tablespoon minced fresh chives
2 eggs, beaten
⅛ teaspoon salt, or to taste
Melted butter or oil

Preheat the oven to 375 degrees. Follow the directions on the phyllo package for thawing and unwrapping the dough. In a medium bowl, mix together the ricotta, mozzarella, nigella, parsley, chives, eggs, and salt.

Working on a sheet of wax paper, layer 4 phyllo sheets on top of one another, brushing each sheet with melted butter or oil. Cut crosswise into 7 equal strips, about 2½ inches wide. One inch from the bottom of each strip, place 1 teaspoon of the filling, a little off center. Make a diagonal fold by bringing the bottom edge up to align with the side edge, creating a triangle. Fold the triangle up and over the horizontal edge across the top. Continue folding the triangle onto itself, much like the formal folding of a flag. Pinch edges and points to seal. Brush the top with butter.

Lay the triangles seam side down, about 1 inch apart, on an ungreased cookie sheet. Bake 15 to 20 minutes, or until golden brown.

MAKES ABOUT 2 DOZEN TRIANGLES

VEGETABLES À LA GRECQUE

You can prepare these marinated vegetables early in the day and refrigerate until ready to serve. A nice way to serve summer produce from your garden.

3½ cups water
6 tablespoons lemon juice
¾ cup dry white wine
½ cup olive oil
1½ teaspoons salt
2 bay leaves
2 cloves garlic, minced
1 shallot or 1 green onion, chopped
6 whole black peppercorns

1 tablespoon minced fresh tarragon,
    or 1 teaspoon dried tarragon, crumbled
2 teaspoons fresh thyme, or 1 teaspoon
    dried thyme, crumbled
About 4 cups of prepared, assorted fresh
    vegetables such as carrots, asparagus,
    zucchini, bell peppers, broccoli,
    and cauliflower

Using a large Dutch oven or other pot, pour in the water and add the lemon juice, wine, oil, salt, and bay leaves. Make a bouquet garni by enclosing the garlic, shallot, peppercorns, tarragon, and thyme in a cheesecloth bag; add to the pan. Bring to a boil and simmer 10 minutes.

Add each vegetable of your choice in sequence and cook each batch until crisp, yet tender. Remove the vegetables when done and set aside. Add the next batch and repeat. Remove the cheesecloth bag and discard the herbs. Simmer the broth until it has reduced to 1 cup; cool the broth slightly, then spoon over the vegetables that have been arranged on a serving platter. Cover with plastic wrap and refrigerate until ready to serve.

MAKES 12 SERVINGS

TARRAGON-MARINATED MUSHROOMS

The dark green color of the herbs provides a stunning contrast to both mushrooms and cauliflower. For even more color, add some finely chopped pimientos.

1 pound mushrooms, cleaned
¾ cup vegetable oil
¼ cup wine vinegar (red or white)
2 tablespoons lemon juice
3 tablespoons minced fresh chives
1 tablespoon minced fresh tarragon,
    or 1 teaspoon dried tarragon, crumbled
1 teaspoon salt
½ teaspoon sugar
½ teaspoon minced fresh dill
1 clove garlic, minced

If the mushrooms are large, halve them and set aside. Combine the oil, vinegar, lemon juice, chives, tarragon, salt, sugar, dill, and garlic in a large lidded container. Add the mushrooms, cover, and shake well. Marinate 4 hours or longer in the refrigerator. Shake occasionally. Served chilled.

VARIATION: *Broccoli (2 stalks) or cauliflower florets (1 head) can be substituted for the mushrooms.*

MAKES 6 SERVINGS

BAY LEAVES

Bay leaves, also called laurel leaves, were symbols of victory, success, and peace, and of excellence in literature and the arts. Hence they became the symbol of the triumphant leader, the honored scholar, or the victorious athlete. Today we refer to one "winning his laurels" as achieving acclaim or success.

CHIVES

Chiues attenuate or make thinne, open, prouoke urine, ingender hotte and grosse vapors and are hurtfull to the eies and braine. They cause troublesome dreames.

TUSSER

HERBED WALNUTS

These tasty morsels can be made ahead and stored in a covered container.
They're nice to have on hand for when company drops in.

4 cups walnut halves
2 tablespoons butter or margarine, melted
1 teaspoon chili powder
¼ teaspoon curry powder

1 tablespoon minced fresh basil
1 tablespoon minced fresh oregano
2 tablespoons minced fresh thyme
2 tablespoons minced fresh marjoram

Add the walnuts to a pot of boiling water; boil for 2 minutes. Drain well, and spread in a single layer on an ungreased baking sheet. Bake at 350 degrees for 12 minutes, until golden brown. Gently toss the walnuts with the melted butter, chili powder, curry powder, basil, oregano, thyme, and marjoram. Cool before serving.

MAKES 4 CUPS

MARJORAM

In Elizabethan times in England, marjoram was one of the strewing herbs scattered on floors to release its sweet fragrance and freshen the air. It was also carried in nosegays.

Crostini

Crostini, a longtime favorite Italian appetizer, is simple to make and can be as light or hearty as you wish. Use fresh sourdough, French, or Italian bread. Cut each loaf into slices to ¼ to ½ inch thick. Cut each slice in half or thirds so that the pieces can be picked up easily with one hand. Slice baguettes at the same thickness, on the diagonal.

The crostini can be toasted, grilled, or sautéed in a little olive oil. Toast for 10 minutes on an ungreased baking sheet in a 325-degree oven. Remove the crostini, rub with a cut clove of garlic, drizzle with a little extra-virgin olive oil, and sprinkle with finely minced fresh herbs. Thyme, basil, oregano, or sweet marjoram are perfect. You could also add some freshly grated pecorino cheese.

TOMATO BASIL CROSTINI

This recipe tastes best when made with garden fresh tomatoes.

3 cups tomatoes, peeled, seeded, and chopped
½ cup chopped fresh basil
2 tablespoons balsamic vinegar
½ teaspoon salt, or to taste
1 ½ cups chopped red onion

½ cup olive oil
1 teaspoon sugar
¼ teaspoon freshly ground black pepper
1 loaf French or Italian bread, sliced ½ inch thick

Combine the tomatoes, basil, balsamic vinegar, salt, red onion, olive oil, sugar, and black pepper in a bowl. Mix until thoroughly blended. Cover and let sit for at least 1 hour.

Just before serving, place 1 tablespoon of the tomato mixture on each bread slice. Arrange slices on a platter and serve. Or, arrange bread slices in a basket or on a plate next to the bowl of tomatoes, allowing your guests to make their own crostini. Serve at room temperature.

MAKES 10 TO 12 SERVINGS

MOZZARELLA, ARUGULA, AND TOMATO CROSTINI

Another recipe to show off your home-grown tomatoes.

3 large tomatoes, cut into
   ¼-inch-thick slices and halved
1 red onion, very thinly sliced
3 tablespoons red wine vinegar
Salt and pepper to taste

4 cups arugula, stemmed,
   coarsely chopped, and packed tightly
8 ounces mozzarella, thinly sliced
1 loaf French or Italian bread,
   sliced ½ inch thick

Combine the tomatoes, red onion, vinegar, salt, and pepper. Marinate for 30 minutes, tossing occasionally. With a slotted spoon, transfer the tomato mixture to a plate. Coat the arugula with the leftover marinade.

Just before serving, assemble the crostini by layering the arugula, a slice of mozzarella, and the tomato mixture on the bread.

SERVES 6 TO 8

Spreads and Fillings

FIVE-HERB FETA SPREAD

Adjust the amounts of herbs to suit your own taste.

4 ounces feta cheese
¼ cup mayonnaise
6 ounces cream cheese, at room temperature
1 clove garlic, minced
1 teaspoon minced fresh basil,
   or ¼ teaspoon dried
1 teaspoon minced fresh thyme,
   or ½ teaspoon dried

1 teaspoon minced fresh dill,
   or ¼ teaspoon dried
1 teaspoon minced fresh marjoram,
   or ½ teaspoon dried
Crackers or lightly toasted
   baguette rounds
Herb sprigs for garnish

In a blender or food processor, combine the feta, mayonnaise, cream cheese, garlic, basil, thyme, dill, and marjoram. Transfer to a serving bowl; cover and refrigerate for at least 2 hours. This spread will keep, covered and refrigerated, for 1 week.

Serve with baguette rounds or crackers and garnished with fresh herbs.

MAKES 1 GENEROUS CUP

MUSHROOM PÂTÉ WITH DRIED CRANBERRIES

Chive flowers make a pretty and crunchy garnish.

1 tablespoon butter
½ cup minced shallots
4 cups portobello mushrooms, chopped
½ cup dry sherry
1 tablespoon minced fresh thyme
3 tablespoons minced fresh parsley
2 tablespoons minced fresh chives, plus additional for garnish
1 cup walnuts, toasted and coarsely chopped
¼ cup dried cranberries, plus additional for garnish
1 teaspoon salt
¼ teaspoon Tabasco
1 (8-ounce) package regular or
    light cream cheese, at room temperature
Cranberries for garnish
Chives for garnish

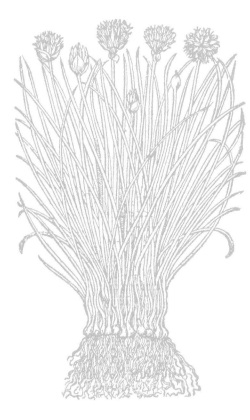

In a large skillet, melt the butter and add the shallots. Cook for 3 minutes, until softened. Add the mushrooms and cook over medium-high heat until the mushrooms release their moisture, about 5 minutes. Add the sherry and cook until most of the liquid has evaporated.

With a mixer on low speed, combine the thyme, parsley, chives, mushroom mixture, walnuts, cranberries, salt, Tabasco, and cream cheese. Mound into a medium bowl or 2 smaller bowls; refrigerate at least 2 hours. When ready to serve, unmold onto a platter and garnish with cranberries and chives. Serve with crackers.

MAKES ABOUT 4 CUPS

HERBED CREAM CHEESE SPREAD

A fine base for canapés or tea sandwiches. Top with thinly sliced cucumber or radish, or a halved cherry tomato.

1 (8-ounce) package cream cheese
¼ cup (2 ounces) butter, at room temperature
1 clove garlic, minced
1 teaspoon minced fresh oregano

1 teaspoon minced fresh dill
1 teaspoon minced fresh basil
1 teaspoon minced fresh thyme

Combine the cream cheese, butter, garlic, oregano, dill, basil, and thyme in a blender or food processor until smooth. Serve with crackers or crostini or fill blanched snow peas with spread.

VARIATION: *Substitute other fresh herbs such as savory, marjoram, or rosemary.*

MAKES 1 GENEROUS CUP

CILANTRO CURRY SPREAD

Use this spread to stuff vegetables such as celery, snow peas, cherry tomatoes, or endive leaves.

1 (8-ounce) package cream cheese,
   regular or light
¾ cup (1 bunch) chopped cilantro,
   plus additional for garnish

2 teaspoons curry powder
2 tablespoons minced fresh chives
1 clove garlic, minced

Bring the cream cheese to room temperature; mix well with the cilantro, curry powder, chives, and garlic. Garnish with cilantro sprigs.

MAKES 1 1/2 CUPS

HERB FILLINGS FOR FRESH VEGETABLES

Herb fillings appeal to diners who prefer to avoid crackers and chips. The fillings can be made ahead of time and, depending on the vegetable, can be filled early in the day, placed on the serving platter, covered with plastic wrap, and refrigerated until serving time. Possible vegetable containers include cherry tomatoes, celery stalks, snow peas, endive, and cucumber rounds cut about ⅜ inch thick. The latter is best done as follows: Score the peel of the cucumber with a fork. Cut off the ends. Cut the cucumber into thirds horizontally, resulting in three 2- to 3-inch cylinders. With a paring knife or small spoon, remove the seeds. Fill the hollow core with the herb mixture. Wrap in plastic wrap and refrigerate. Just before serving, slice the cucumber into rounds. Place the cucumber cylinders on a plate lined with lettuce leaves and garnish each slice with a sprig of fresh herb or an edible flower petal.

These fillings can also be converted into dips by thinning the mixture with a little milk, wine, or juice. Use the dips with jicama, bell pepper, carrot, raw broccoli, and cauliflower florets.

Dill and Shrimp

Combine 1 (8-ounce) package cream cheese, 1 tablespoon minced fresh dill, ¼ cup catsup, and 2 ounces cooked, chopped bay shrimp.

Sage and Garlic

Combine 1 cup cottage cheese, 1 clove garlic, pressed, 2 tablespoons minced fresh sage, ½ teaspoon salt, and 1 tablespoon snipped fresh chives.

Tuna and Herbs

Combine 1 (13-ounce) can tuna, 2 finely chopped hard-boiled eggs, 2 teaspoons lemon juice, ¼ cup mayonnaise, and ¼ cup mixed herbs such as parsley, chives, tarragon, dill, lovage, chervil, and marjoram.

Tarragon and Chervil

Combine 1 (8-ounce) package cream cheese, 2 cloves garlic, pressed, 1 tablespoon minced fresh tarragon, ⅓ cup minced fresh parsley, 1 tablespoon minced fresh chervil, and ⅓ cup chopped green onion.

Caraway-Herb

Combine 1 (8-ounce) package cream cheese, 1 clove garlic, pressed, 1 tablespoon minced fresh basil, 1 teaspoon minced fresh dill, 2 tablespoons minced fresh chives, ½ teaspoon caraway seeds, and ½ teaspoon minced lemon zest.

Blue Cheese and Dill

Combine 1 cup sour cream, ⅓ cup crumbled blue cheese, ⅓ cup minced fresh parsley, 1 teaspoon minced fresh dill, 1 tablespoon lemon juice, 1 clove garlic, pressed, 2 green onions, chopped, and 1 teaspoon salt.

GORGONZOLA HERB SPREAD

Dried herbs are excellent in this easy-to-make spread.

6 ounces Gorgonzola cheese,
   at room temperature
12 ounces cream cheese, at room temperature

½ teaspoon dried oregano
½ teaspoon dried basil
½ teaspoon dried summer savory
1 baguette
¼ cup (2 ounces) butter, softened

Heat the broiler. Beat the cheeses until fluffy. Place in a serving dish and set aside. Combine the oregano, basil, and savory. Slice the baguette in half horizontally. Spread with butter and sprinkle the herb blend over the top. Broil until lightly browned.

To serve, cut the bread into wedges. Serve hot cheese mixture to spread on portions.

❧ VARIATION: *Blue cheese can be substituted for the Gorgonzola cheese.*

MAKES 6 TO 8 SERVINGS

SESAME HERB SPREAD

A good recipe for using up leftover bread slices.

½ cup (¼ pound) butter or margarine,
   at room temperature
2 tablespoons sesame seeds
¼ teaspoon marjoram
1 tablespoon chopped fresh chives
¼ teaspoon dried basil
¼ teaspoon dried rosemary
10 slices of thin bread, cut diagonally in half

Combine the butter with the sesame seeds, marjoram, chives, basil, and rosemary. Spread on the slices of bread and place on a cookie sheet. Bake at 325 degrees for 15 minutes.

❧ VARIATION: *This mixture can also be used with a loaf of French bread, cut diagonally, wrapped in foil, and heated in the oven.*

MAKES 20 SERVINGS

FRESH HERB SPREAD

Chopping these fresh herbs is only the prelude. The real joy comes in eating the bread with the spread.

½ cup (¼ pound) butter or margarine
2 tablespoons chopped fresh parsley
1 tablespoon chopped green onion,
 white and green parts
1 tablespoon chopped lovage
1 teaspoon chopped fresh oregano
1 teaspoon chopped fresh thyme
1 teaspoon chopped fresh rosemary
1 teaspoon chopped fresh basil
2 tablespoons lemon juice
Salt
1 medium French bread loaf

Melt or soften the butter. Add the parsley, green onion, and lovage. Blend in the oregano, thyme, rosemary, basil, lemon juice, and salt. Cut the French bread into ½-inch-thick slices. Spread the butter mixture generously over one side of each slice. Put the slices together again to form the loaf, and wrap securely in foil. Bake at 350 degrees for 35 minutes. Serve hot.

MAKES 12 SERVINGS

THYME

In the Middle Ages, perhaps because of the business of the bees in a patch of thyme flowers, thyme also became the symbol of energy or activity. Honey made from bees who worked the fields of wild thyme was considered to be the best kind.

Plate 236.

Chervil.   { 1. Flower.   2. Flower Enlarg'd.   3. Seed Vessel open.   4. Seed. }   *Chaerefolium.*

Eliz Blackwell delin. sculp et Pinx.

CHAPTER 4
Salads and Salad Dressings

Herb Vinegars

Get creative with easy, inexpensive, useful herb vinegars. First, you'll need a supply of fresh herbs; wine or cider vinegars lend their own flavor, but clear distilled vinegar allows the herbs to shine through. If you're going to use red basil, it is best to use only the distilled vinegar. The red (sometimes called purple) basil lends its wonderful fruity flavor to the product, along with its beautiful claret shade of red. Decorative clear bottles enhance the presentation, but any clean jar will do. The containers do not need to be sterilized, but they should be scrupulously cleaned, and always rinse and pat the fresh herbs dry before using.

Place the herbs in a jar or bottle, add the vinegar, and cap. Just that simple! How much of an herb should you use? There are no hard and fast rules here. Start with 2 or 3 sprigs, about 4 to 6 inches long. Adjust the quantity of herbs to taste.

Put the containers in a cool, dark place for 2 to 3 weeks and shake them every few days. When the time is up, you can use them as is, or you can remove the original herbs and replace them with a few fresh sprigs for decoration.

Do not heat the vinegar, or it will become cloudy. The flavor is not affected, but a clear liquid is more attractive.

Use any of the following herbs alone or in combination, including the leaves and flowers of chives, garlic chives, dill, fennel, and any of the basils.

BORAGE   BURNET   CHERVIL   FRENCH TARRAGON
LEMON BALM   LEMON GRASS   LOVAGE   MEXICAN TARRAGON
MINT   OREGANO   ROSEMARY   THYME

You can also add peppercorns, garlic, or orange or lemon zest for flavor and decoration.

For a vinaigrette or marinade, use various kinds of vinegars and oils in a formula of three parts oil to one part herb vinegar. For mayonnaise-based dressings, to each cup of store-bought mayonnaise, add ¼ to ⅓ cup fresh minced herbs or 1 to 2 tablespoons dried herbs, depending on their strength.

Salad Herbs

When adding fresh herbs to salads, torn or shredded basil is a great way to start. Don't limit yourself to common sweet basil—try lemon basil, cinnamon basil, anise basil, or any of the other fifteen or more kinds of basil. These herbs can also be minced fresh and tossed into a salad:

CHERVIL   CHIVES   CILANTRO   DILL
GARLIC CHIVES   LOVAGE   PARSLEY   SALAD BURNET

Edible Flowers

To add color, sparkle, and flavor to a salad, consider any of the flowers listed below. Be sure you pick them from plants that have not been treated with pesticides or fungicides.

ARUGULA   BORAGE   CALENDULA (PETALS)   CHIVES
COMMON SAGE   DAYLILIES   GARLIC CHIVES   NASTURTIUMS
PINKS   ROSEMARY   ROSE PETALS   VIOLETS

 **CHERVIL**

The seeds eaten as a sallad whiles they are yet green, with oile, vineger, and pepper, exceed all other sallads by many

degrees, both in pleasantnesse of taste, sweetnesse of smell, and wholsomnesse for the cold and feeble stomacke.

GERARD

MESCLUN

Mesclun consists of various kinds of lettuce, endive, chervil, chicory or radicchio, arugula, and whatever other greens are available. The dressing for such a delicate combination should be a light vinaigrette to prevent overpowering the many other colors, textures, and flavors in this exciting, variable mixture.

TOSSED GREEN SALAD WITH HERBS

Refreshing on a hot summer day, this big, tossed green salad has lots of fresh herbs cut into it. Place a ring of chives or garlic chive flowers around the rim of the serving bowl.

1 head romaine or other type of lettuce
2 medium garden fresh tomatoes
1 Japanese cucumber
1 or 2 cloves garlic
½ cup fresh mixed herbs such as chives,
    garlic chives, sweet basil, French tarragon,
    sorrel, chervil, or flat-leaf parsley
1½ tablespoons lemon juice
2 tablespoons red wine vinegar
6 to 8 tablespoons light olive oil
Salt and pepper to taste
1 avocado
1 hard-boiled egg, riced or chopped fine
Fresh basil leaves for garnish

Tear the lettuce into small pieces and chill. Cut the tomatoes into bite-sized pieces. If they are juicy, drain well. Peel the cucumber and slice thinly.

About 30 minutes before serving, rub a salad bowl with a cut clove of garlic. Cut the herbs of your choice into the bowl with scissors and squeeze the lemon juice over them; gently stir. Let set a few minutes. Combine the vinegar and olive oil in a small bowl.

Add the lettuce, tomatoes, and cucumbers to the herbs, sprinkle with salt and pepper, and toss with the dressing. Peel and slice the avocado onto the salad. Garnish with egg and basil leaves.

MAKES 6 TO 8 SERVINGS

LETTUCE

(Letuce) the same taken in the same manner (eaten rawe in salads) causeth sound and sweete sleepe, it maketh the belly good and soft, and engendereth abundance of milke: it is very good for suche as cannot take their rest, and for Nurses, and for suche as give sucke, whiche have but small store of milke, but for that purpose it is better before it begynneth to shoot forth his stalkes: for whom it putteth foorth his stalkes it waxeth bitter and is not so good in meates as before.

DODOENS

ARUGULA AND WARM PONZU SALMON SALAD

Perfect for a summer luncheon on the patio.

4 salmon steaks

Marinade
¼ cup soy sauce
¼ cup citrus seasoned sauce

Ponzu Dressing
2 tablespoons soy sauce
2 tablespoons citrus seasoned sauce
3 tablespoons olive oil

Salad
4 bunches arugula
1 English cucumber, thinly sliced
½ carrot, grated
3 tablespoons sliced fresh chives

ARUGULA

Rocket is a good sallet herbe, if it be eaten with Lettuce, Purslane, and such cold herbes; for being so eaten it is good and wholesome for the stomacke, and causeth that such cold herbes do not over-coole the same: otherwise, to be eaten alone, it causeth head-ache, and heateth too much.

GERARD

Combine the soy and citrus sauces for the marinade, and marinate the salmon for at least 1 hour. To make the dressing, combine the soy sauce, citrus sauce, and olive oil and set aside. Broil the salmon 6 minutes on each side, until it is cooked through.

Toss the arugula, cucumber, carrot, and chives with the dressing. Arrange the warm salmon on top and serve.

NOTE: *Citrus seasoned sauce is available in Asian supermarkets.*

MAKES 4 SERVINGS

ARUGULA SALAD WITH SUGARED NUTS AND GORGONZOLA

Arugula makes a lovely salad to serve in autumn with ripe pears and apples.

Sugared Nuts
2 tablespoons butter, melted
2 tablespoons brown sugar
½ cup walnuts or pecans

Salad
4 bunches arugula, stemmed and torn
2 apples, unpeeled, cored, thinly sliced
2 pears, unpeeled, cored, thinly sliced
4 ounces Gorgonzola cheese, crumbled

Dressing

½ cup virgin olive oil

⅓ cup balsamic vinegar

1 teaspoon lemon juice

1 shallot, minced

1 clove garlic, crushed

½ teaspoon nigella seeds

Salt and pepper to taste

Preheat the oven to 350 degrees. Line a baking sheet with aluminum foil. Heat and stir the butter and sugar in a heavy skillet over low heat, until the sugar dissolves. Increase the heat to medium, add the nuts, and stir to coat well. Spread in a single layer on the baking sheet. Bake for 10 to 15 minutes. Stir frequently. Transfer the nuts to another sheet of foil to cool completely. Set aside.

In a small bowl, combine the olive oil, vinegar, lemon juice, shallot, garlic, nigella seeds, salt, and pepper. Place the arugula, apples, pears, and Gorgonzola cheese in a serving bowl. Add the sugared nuts and toss. Add the dressing and toss again to combine.

MAKES 4 TO 6 SERVINGS

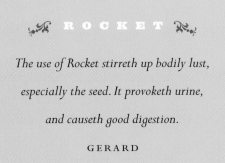

❧ R O C K E T ❧

The use of Rocket stirreth up bodily lust,

especially the seed. It provoketh urine,

and causeth good digestion.

GERARD

SPINACH SALAD WITH BASIL AND FETA

The crunchy walnuts combine nicely with the feta and avocado.

Dressing

½ cup olive oil

¼ cup wine vinegar

2 teaspoons sugar

2 cloves garlic, minced

½ teaspoon salt

½ teaspoon pepper

Salad

1 bunch spinach, finely chopped

1 avocado, cubed

½ medium red onion, chopped

½ cup minced fresh basil

½ cup crumbled feta cheese

½ cup coarsely chopped walnuts

Combine the olive oil, vinegar, sugar, garlic, salt, and pepper in a small bowl. Toss the spinach, avocado, red onion, basil, feta, and walnuts in a large bowl. Pour as much of the dressing over the salad as desired and toss.

MAKES 4 TO 6 SERVINGS

ELEGANT FALL FRUIT SALAD

Loosely based on the Waldorf-Astoria Hotel's famous salad.

Dressing

1 cup plain yogurt
1 tablespoon fennel seeds, crushed
1 teaspoon sugar
2 tablespoons Grand Marnier
¼ cup chopped fresh mint leaves

Salad

3 stalks celery, chopped
1 cup chopped walnuts, toasted
1 cup red seedless grapes, sliced
2 apples, cored and diced
1 small head Bibb lettuce

Combine the yogurt, fennel seeds, sugar, Grand Marnier, and mint in a bowl. Toss the celery, walnuts, grapes, and apples with the dressing. Arrange the lettuce leaves on a serving platter and top with salad.
🌿 VARIATION: *Look for some fresh sweet fennel at the market; use the stalks, thinly sliced, in place of the celery. Or, add ¼ cup chopped lovage leaves for a celery flavor.*

MAKES 4 SERVINGS

APPLE, PECAN, AND DRIED CHERRY SALAD

This nutty fruit salad is paired with Stilton cheese and a curry dressing.

Dressing

1 large shallot, minced
2 tablespoons mango or ginger chutney
3 tablespoons light wine vinegar
⅓ cup vegetable oil
¼ cup apple juice
2 teaspoons curry powder
¼ teaspoon salt
Freshly ground pepper to taste

Salad

1 cup pecan halves, toasted
6 cups mixed baby greens
½ cup dried cherries
½ cup crumbled Stilton cheese
¼ cup julienned fresh basil
2 tablespoons minced fresh mint leaves
2 tablespoons minced fresh cilantro
2 medium red-skinned tart apples, halved, cored, and thinly sliced

> **FENNEL**
>
> *The leaves, or rather the seeds, boiled in water, stays the hiccough, and takes away the loathings, which oftentimes happen to the stomachs of sick and feverish persons, and allys the heat thereof.*
>
> CULPEPER

To make the curry dressing, blend the shallot, chutney, vinegar, oil, apple juice, curry powder, salt, and pepper in a food processor or blender until smooth. The dressing can be made 2 days ahead and refrigerated. Bring to room temperature and stir before using.

To toast the pecans, spread them in a single layer on a baking sheet. Bake in a 350-degree oven until the nuts turn slightly deeper brown and fragrant, about 10 minutes.

Reserve 4 pecans for the garnish. Combine the remaining pecans, greens, cherries, cheese, basil, mint, and cilantro in a large bowl. Add ¾ cup of the curry dressing. Toss well. Add more dressing if desired. Adjust the seasonings to taste.

Divide evenly between 4 chilled serving plates. Arrange the apple slices on the salads. Drizzle any remaining dressing over the apples. Center the reserved pecans on each salad. Serve immediately.

MAKES 4 SERVINGS

HERBED ORZO SALAD

Use orzo with fresh herbs and feta cheese to make this light, delicious pasta salad.
Top with chopped tomatoes or red pepper to add color.

1 pound orzo
¼ cup olive oil
¼ cup lemon juice
2 tablespoons white wine vinegar
6 tablespoons minced fresh chives
¼ cup minced fresh oregano

4 teaspoons minced fresh dill
8 ounces feta cheese, diced
1 cup chopped yellow bell pepper
 (1 medium)
Salt and pepper to taste

Cook the orzo according to the package directions. Rinse in cool water and drain well. Place the orzo in a large bowl and immediately stir in the olive oil to prevent sticking. Add the lemon juice, vinegar, chives, oregano, dill, feta, bell pepper, salt, and pepper; stir to combine. The salad can be served immediately or refrigerated for later use. Bring to room temperature before serving. Can be made a day in advance.

MAKES 6 TO 8 SERVINGS

DILL

The oil that is made of dyll is good
to be given unto them that are weary in
winter for it softeneth and moisteneth.

TURNER

MINTED APRICOT RICE SALAD

A delicious salad to take on summer picnics, it contains nothing that can spoil if not refrigerated.

1 cup finely chopped dried apricots

2 tablespoons triple sec

Grated zest and juice of 1 orange

1 cup pecan halves

1 cup chopped dates

1½ cups cooked and chilled wild rice

1½ cups cooked and chilled white or brown rice

¾ cup chopped fresh mint leaves

2 tablespoons light olive oil

Salt and pepper to taste

Combine the apricots, triple sec, orange zest, and juice in a small saucepan. Bring to a boil. Remove from heat, set aside, and let cool completely.

Place the pecans on a baking sheet and roast them at 350 degrees until lightly browned. Cool completely.

Combine the apricots and liquid, pecans, dates, wild rice, white or brown rice, and mint leaves, tossing lightly. Chill thoroughly. When ready to serve, combine the mixture with olive oil. Season to taste with salt and pepper.

MAKES 6 TO 8 SERVINGS

TABBOULEH

*A particularly refreshing summer salad. Scoop and eat with leaves
of romaine lettuce or with wedges of pita bread, fresh or toasted.*

1 cup cracked wheat

1 cup boiling water

3 Roma tomatoes, diced

½ cucumber, peeled and diced

1 cup minced fresh parsley

⅓ cup minced fresh spearmint

1 clove garlic, minced

½ cup finely chopped green onion

⅓ cup lemon juice

⅓ cup virgin olive oil

¼ teaspoon salt

¼ teaspoon freshly ground pepper

4 ounces feta cheese, crumbled

Place the cracked wheat in a large bowl and pour the boiling water over it. Cover and let stand 1 hour, tossing twice. Drain well in a colander. Return to the bowl. Add the tomatoes, cucumber, parsley, spearmint, garlic, green onion, lemon juice, olive oil, salt, and pepper. Mix well but gently. Refrigerate for at least 3 hours. Top with feta cheese just before serving.

❋ VARIATION: *Minced fresh dill or basil can be added with the other herbs.*

MAKES 6 SERVINGS

Plate 290.

Mint.

Eliz. Blackwell delin. sculp. et Pinx.

1. Flower.
2. Flower separate.
3. Calix.
4. Seed.

Mentha.

HERB CUSTARD CUBES

12 tarragon leaves and 1 tablespoon parsley
1½ tablespoons chives and
1½ tablespoons parsley

9 sage leaves and 2 tablespoons chives
1 tablespoon each of lemon thyme,
parsley, and chives

Beat together 2 whole eggs, 2 egg yolks, 1 cup milk, and ⅛ teaspoon salt. Add any one mixture of the minced fresh herbs listed above.

Pour the mixture into six custard cups and place them in a pan of hot water. Bake in a 350-degree oven for 40 minutes. Remove, cool, and refrigerate until ready to serve. Carefully remove each custard and place in a bowl of hot broth to serve. Instead of using custard cups, you can also pour the herb-egg liquid into a straight-sided baking dish set in a pan of hot water. Use a dish large enough so liquid is only to a depth of ½ inch. Bake 45 to 50 minutes until set. When cool, cut into cubes. Add to broth when serving.

HERB EGG FLOWERS

Beat together 2 eggs and then add ¼ cup of any of the following minced fresh herbs, or a combination of any: chives, garlic chives, sweet marjoram, parsley, tarragon, lemon thyme, lemon basil, or lovage. Bring 1 quart chicken broth to a simmer. While stirring the broth, pour in the herb-egg mixture in a steady stream. Simmer 1 minute and serve.

HERBED CROUTONS

Cut stale bread into ½-inch cubes. Spread 2 cups of bread cubes on a cookie sheet and bake in a 400-degree oven for 10 to 15 minutes until bread is dry. Add 1 to 2 tablespoons of minced fresh herbs to ½ cup melted butter. Use your favorite herb butter combination. Toss the bread cubes in the herb butter until all are coated. Sauté them in a non-stick pan until golden brown on all sides. Store in a covered container for up to 1 day without refrigeration. For more than a day, refrigerate until needed.

GARLIC CROUTONS

Cut bread into ½-inch slices. Spread one side with herb or garlic butter. Cut into ½-inch cubes. Toast in an ungreased heavy skillet over medium heat until golden brown, about 5 to 7 minutes.

HERB TOAST

Slice a loaf of good French or Italian bread into ½- to ¾-inch thicknesses. Spread with your favorite herb butter and, if desired, sprinkle with a little grated Parmesan cheese. Just before serving, place on a cookie sheet and put the bread slices under the broiler until heated through and somewhat "bubbly." Place one slice of herb toast in each soup bowl and ladle soup gently over it.

HERB BUTTER

Float a shaped herb butter slice on a cup of broth. For recipes, see page 2.

PESTO

Known as *pistou* in French, a swirl of pesto can add a burst of flavor to a soup or broth. Add just before serving.

Soups
HERBED VICHYSSOISE

Extremely light and refreshing in summer, this soup is pale green with darker flecks of herbs.

½ pound potatoes	1½ tablespoons minced fresh dill
2 tablespoons vegetable oil	Zest of 1 lemon
½ cup minced green onion	2 cups chicken broth
⅓ cup minced fresh garlic chives	1 cup milk
½ cup minced fresh flat-leaf parsley	Salt and pepper to taste
2 tablespoons minced fresh tarragon	Mixed minced fresh herbs for garnish

Cook the potatoes in boiling water until tender. Set aside to cool. In a medium saucepan, heat the oil over medium-low heat. Add the green onion, garlic chives, parsley, tarragon, dill, and lemon zest. Cook for 2 minutes. Add the chicken broth, bring to a boil, and cook 2 minutes. Set aside to cool.

In a blender or food processor, purée the herb mixture with the milk and potatoes in two batches. Cover and chill. Just before serving, taste for salt and pepper. Garnish with minced herbs.

MAKES 4 SERVINGS

CHILLED CORN SOUP WITH BASIL SWIRL

A basil purée is swirled into this creamy soup just before serving, adding a burst of color and flavor.

6 ears sweet corn, shucked

¼ cup plus 2 tablespoons olive oil

1 ½ cups chopped onion

1 clove garlic, minced

4 cups chicken broth

3 cups water

½ cup cream

White pepper to taste

Salt to taste

1 cup packed basil leaves

Cut the corn kernels off the cobs and reserve the cobs. Heat 2 tablespoons of the oil in a large saucepan over medium-low heat. Cook the onion and garlic 5 minutes, until the onion is soft. Add the reserved corncobs, broth, and water. Bring to a boil over medium heat and simmer 10 minutes.

Add the corn kernels, simmer 15 minutes, and discard the corncobs. Stir in the cream, white pepper, and salt; simmer 5 minutes. Remove from heat and let cool. In a blender or food processor, purée the mixture in batches and transfer to a bowl. Cover the soup and chill at least 3 hours, or up to 24 hours.

In a food processor, purée the basil and the remaining ¼ cup olive oil with salt to taste. Divide the soup among individual soup bowls and swirl some of the basil purée into each serving.

MAKES 6 SERVINGS

CREAM OF SORREL SOUP

Sorrel is easy to grow and prolific, with a lemony, tart flavor that goes well with the creamy chicken base of this soup, which can be served hot or cold. A popular soup at the Huntington restaurant.

6 ounces fresh sorrel

2 tablespoons butter

2 quarts chicken broth

4 egg yolks

¾ cup cream, heavy or light

½ cup minced fresh chervil for garnish

⅓ cup port wine, for chilled version only (optional)

Stem the sorrel and cut into thin strips crosswise. Melt the butter in a large saucepan over low heat. Add the sorrel and cook until it is reduced by one half. Add the chicken broth and simmer for 15 minutes.

Mix the egg yolks and cream in a large bowl. Just before serving, pour a little of the hot soup into the egg cream mixture, stirring vigorously to blend. Pour this mixture back into the saucepan. Cook gently over medium heat, about 5 minutes, stirring constantly, until the soup thickens and coats the back of a spoon. Just before serving, sprinkle with the chervil.

To serve cold, refrigerate several hours. Add the port wine just before serving.

MAKES 8 SERVINGS

CREAM OF CARROT AND LOVAGE SOUP

Lovage, a lesser-known herb, has a strong, celery-like scent and a bright, clean flavor.
Here it blends well with parsley and dill, yet none of these overpower the essential carrot flavor.

4 tablespoons butter
¾ cup chopped onion
6 carrots, peeled and sliced
⅓ cup chopped lovage leaves
2 medium potatoes, peeled and diced
⅓ cup minced fresh flat-leaf parsley

5 cups chicken broth
1 (3-inch) sprig fresh dill
1 cup light cream or half-and-half
Salt and pepper to taste
Ground fresh nutmeg (optional)

Melt the butter in a large saucepan over medium heat. Add the onion, carrots, and lovage. Cook 10 to 15 minutes, stirring occasionally. Add the potatoes and parsley; stir until coated. Add the chicken broth and cook, partially covered, until the potatoes are almost tender, about 10 to 12 minutes. Add the sprig of fresh dill and cook another 5 minutes, until the potatoes are completely tender.

Remove from heat and let cool for a few minutes. Purée in batches in a blender or food processor. Return the puréed soup to the saucepan. Stir in the light cream and season to taste with salt and pepper. This soup can be served hot or cold. Chill if serving cold, or reheat without boiling to serve hot. Sprinkle with a light dusting of ground nutmeg, if desired.

MAKES 4 TO 6 SERVINGS

> **DILL**
>
> *Sleepe to cause, weare a garland of greene Dill*
>
> *to the head. . . . anoint the head with oyle.*
>
> LANGHAM

CILANTRO AND LIME SOUP

Tasty and good when avocados are in season.

2 tablespoons olive oil
1 cup chopped onion
3 cloves garlic, chopped
6 cups chicken broth
1 tablespoon chili powder

1½ cups cooked chicken, diced
1 cup frozen or fresh corn
1 cup diced and seeded tomatoes
½ bunch fresh cilantro, chopped,
    plus additional for optional garnish
¼ cup lime juice
1 avocado, diced, for garnish (optional)
Garlic croutons (optional)

CORIANDER

Coriander/cilantro was introduced to China about 600 A.D. and was used in both cooking and medicine because people thought it had the power of conferring immortality.

Heat the oil in a large saucepan. Cook the onion and garlic until golden. Add the chicken broth, chili powder, chicken, corn, tomatoes, cilantro, and lime juice. Cook until heated through. Garnish with chopped cilantro, diced avocado, or garlic croutons (see garnishes).

MAKES 6 SERVINGS

STONE SOUP

Remember the fairy tale entitled "Stone Soup"? You don't need a famine, or even a stone, to try this tasty soup.

1 clean stone (optional)
8 cups water
3 fresh sage leaves
5 leaflets of fresh lovage
1 (3-inch) sprig fresh marjoram
2 large heads (40 cloves) garlic,
    peeled and coarsely chopped
2 bay leaves

3 (3-inch) sprigs fresh thyme or lemon thyme
2 whole cloves
Pinch of saffron or ground turmeric
1½ teaspoons salt
3 egg yolks
¼ cup extra-virgin olive oil
6 to 8 toasted French bread slices
1 cup Parmesan cheese

Put the stone in a large saucepan; add the water and bring to a boil. Add the sage, lovage, marjoram, garlic, bay leaves, thyme, cloves, saffron or turmeric, and salt. Simmer, uncovered, 20 to 30 minutes. Remove the stone. Strain the herbs.

When almost ready to serve the soup, whirl the egg yolks in a blender until pale and creamy. While the motor is running, add small amounts of olive oil, a little at a time, until thickened. Stir in some of the hot soup, then add this mixture to the rest of the soup to thicken it.

Place a toasted bread slice in each soup bowl. Sprinkle with Parmesan cheese. Ladle soup over the bread.

🌿 VARIATION: *It can be "fancied up" in many ways: add rice, pasta, beans, or barley instead of bread to the simmering soup and cook until tender. Add sliced mushrooms or vegetables such as carrot, celery, corn, peas, or green beans; simmer until done. Or, add chicken. Drizzle some more beaten egg into the simmering soup, stirring gently. Serve hot.*

MAKES 6 SERVINGS

STONE SOUP

Once upon a time, during a great famine, a peasant woman told her neighbors that she could make soup from a stone. To prove it, she selected and washed a nice big stone and put it into a large pot filled with water. "If only I had some garlic, it would be so much better!" she sighed. A neighbor woman remembered that she had a few bulbs of garlic; they were soon added to the pot. "Ah, a little bit of sage would be so good to add," she remarked. Another neighbor brought her a few leaves to drop in. And so it went with a few more herbs. After it simmered for a while, the woman invited her hungry neighbors to bring their bowls and any scraps of bread and cheese they had. That night they feasted with great merriment on the wonderful and miraculous Stone Soup.

LETTUCE AND TARRAGON SOUP

Certain to please your guests, this delicately flavored soup is perfect for a formal dinner or a spring luncheon.

⅓ cup minced onion
1 tablespoon butter
1 head iceberg lettuce,
    torn into small pieces
1 teaspoon minced fresh tarragon,
    or ½ teaspoon dried
1 tablespoon flour

6 cups chicken broth
½ cup heavy cream
1 teaspoon salt
¼ teaspoon white pepper
¼ teaspoon freshly grated nutmeg
½ cucumber, peeled, seeded,
    and chopped

Sauté the onion in butter in a medium saucepan until the onion is transparent. Stir in the lettuce and tarragon and cook over low heat until the lettuce is soft. Remove from heat. Stir in the flour and gradually add 2 cups of the chicken broth. Return to heat and simmer for 25 minutes. Remove from heat to cool for 5 minutes. Purée the lettuce mixture in a blender or food processor.

Return the puréed soup to the saucepan. Stir in the remaining 4 cups chicken broth, cream, salt, white pepper, and nutmeg until well blended. Stir in the cucumber. Reheat over low heat without bringing to a boil. Serve immediately. **MAKES 4 TO 6 SERVINGS**

YOGURT, SPINACH, AND SORREL SOUP

Fresh herbs highlight this soup that can be served hot or cold.

4 cups chicken broth

2 cups plain yogurt

1½ tablespoons flour

Salt and pepper to taste

1 cup minced fresh spinach

2 cups minced fresh sorrel

3 green onions, white parts only, minced

2 tablespoons minced fresh dill

2 tablespoons minced fresh cilantro

2 tablespoons butter, at room temperature

3 tablespoons minced fresh mint leaves

¼ teaspoon cayenne

Bring the chicken broth to a simmer in a large saucepan. Whisk the yogurt and flour together in a medium bowl; whisk 1 cup hot broth into the yogurt mixture. Return the mixture to the saucepan; add salt and pepper to taste.

Add the spinach and sorrel to the soup; simmer 8 minutes. Add the green onion, dill, and cilantro; simmer for 1 minute. Purée in a blender until smooth.

Mix the butter with the mint and cayenne. Serve the soup hot with a dollop of the mint butter, or serve cold with a sprinkle of dill and chopped green onion.

VARIATION: *For a thicker soup, add ½ cup cooked yellow split peas to the broth before puréeing.*

MAKES 6 SERVINGS

MINT

The nymph Menthe was a lovely daughter of a river god who was encouraged not to stray too far from the protection of her father. Nevertheless, Pluto discovered her and fell madly in love with her. When his wife found out, she decided to cool his passion by changing her rival into a plant. The plant, which we call mint, still prefers areas close to water.

Plate 230.

Sorrel.

1. *Flower.*
2. *Flower separate.*
3. *Seed.*

Eliz. Blackwell delin. sculp: et Pinx.

Acetosa.

AUTUMN APPLE SOUP

A lovely soup to make when "the frost is on the pumpkin."
Its heavenly aroma will scent your home better than any potpourri.

½ cup chopped onion
2 tablespoons butter
2 teaspoons curry powder
1 tablespoon flour
  3 cups chicken broth
    1 ½ pounds apples, peeled,
      cored, and chopped

1 teaspoon lemon juice
1 tablespoon chopped fresh mint
½ cup light cream
½ teaspoon salt
¼ teaspoon white pepper
4 to 6 thin lemon slices
4 to 6 fresh sprigs mint

Sauté the onion in butter in a large saucepan until the onion is transparent, but not browned. Stir in the curry powder and cook 1 minute. Stir in the flour. Gradually add the chicken broth, stirring constantly. Bring the mixture to a boil. Add the apples, and bring back to a boil. Reduce the heat, cover, and simmer for 15 minutes. Remove from heat and let cool 5 minutes.

Pureé the soup, lemon juice, and mint in a blender or food processor. Return the puréed mixture to the saucepan and stir in the cream, salt, and white pepper. Reheat the soup without bringing it to a boil.

Serve immediately, garnishing each serving with a lemon slice and a sprig of mint.

MAKES 4 TO 6 SERVINGS

CARROT SOUP WITH HUNTINGTON HERBS

Frequently served in the Huntington restaurant, this soup uses fresh herbs from the adjacent herb garden.

2 tablespoons butter
½ cup chopped onion
1 clove garlic, chopped
1 leek, white part only, chopped
8 cups chicken broth
8 carrots, sliced
2 large potatoes, peeled and sliced

Salt and pepper to taste
6 (4-inch) sprigs fresh thyme,
  or 1 tablespoon dried
1 tablespoon chopped fresh parsley
1 tablespoon chopped fresh chives
Chive florets for garnish

Melt the butter in a large saucepan over medium heat. Add the onion, garlic, and leek; cook until golden. Add the chicken broth, carrots, and potatoes. Add salt and pepper to taste. Cook until the carrots and potatoes are almost tender. Add the thyme, parsley, and chives and cook 5 more minutes.

Purée in a blender or food processor. Taste for salt and pepper. Serve garnished with chive florets.

MAKES 6 SERVINGS

HERBED BUTTERNUT SQUASH SOUP

Wonderful to prepare during the golden days of autumn.

2 tablespoons butter
1 cup chopped onion
1 clove garlic, chopped
8 large fresh sage leaves, chopped
About 15 (3-inch) sprigs thyme
   or lemon thyme
Zest of 1 lemon, chopped
4 cups chicken broth

3 cups peeled and cubed butternut squash
   (about 1 ½ pounds)
Salt and white pepper to taste
2 ounces Roquefort cheese,
   crumbled (optional)
½ cup chopped walnuts or
   sliced almonds (optional)

Melt the butter in a large saucepan over medium heat. Add the onion and garlic; cook until golden, stirring occasionally, about 5 to 10 minutes. Add the sage, thyme, lemon zest, chicken broth, and squash. Bring to a boil; reduce heat and simmer until the squash is tender, about 20 to 30 minutes.

Discard the thyme stems. Purée the soup in batches in a blender or food processor until smooth. Season to taste with salt and white pepper.

The soup can be refrigerated and reheated when ready to serve. Garnish each serving with crumbled Roquefort cheese and nuts if desired.

MAKES 4 SERVINGS

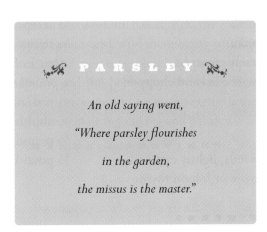

PARSLEY

An old saying went,

"Where parsley flourishes

in the garden,

the missus is the master."

SPICY COCONUT SOUP WITH CHICKEN BALLS

Use the white base of lemon grass in this soup, and save the coarser green part to flavor beverages, but remove them before serving.

½ teaspoon fennel seeds
½ teaspoon cumin seeds
½ teaspoon coriander seeds
3 tablespoons olive oil
1 leek, thinly sliced
2 medium carrots, thinly sliced
1 red onion, thinly sliced
2 bay leaves
1 green or red chili, unseeded, sliced into rings
1 tablespoon chopped fresh ginger
1 stalk lemon grass, finely chopped
6 cloves garlic, minced
1 (13½-ounce) can coconut milk
4 cans water
2 skinless chicken breasts, cubed
½ cup chopped mint leaves
2 tablespoons Thai fish sauce (nam pla)
1 bunch cilantro, chopped
¼ cup lime juice

Toast the fennel, cumin, and coriander seeds in a small skillet over medium heat until fragrant, about 2 minutes; crush lightly. Heat the olive oil in a large saucepan; add the leek, carrots, red onion, bay leaves, chili, ginger, lemon grass, toasted spices, and half of the garlic. Add the coconut milk and water. Bring to a boil and simmer, uncovered, for 20 minutes.

Meanwhile, place the chicken, the rest of the garlic, mint, 2 teaspoons of the fish sauce, and a third of the cilantro in a food processor; mince finely. Chill 20 to 30 minutes and shape into 30 balls. Add to the soup with the remaining fish sauce and simmer 15 minutes.

Just before serving, add the lime juice and the rest of the cilantro.

🌿 VARIATION: *Garnish with rings of red chili if you want the soup to be really spicy.*

MAKES 6 SERVINGS

FRAGRANT SAUSAGE AND BARLEY SOUP

Fresh marjoram gives this hearty soup a heady fragrance.

7 ounces smoked sausage or kielbasa, cooked
3 quarts chicken or vegetable broth
1 cup pearl barley
2 large bay leaves
2 tablespoons extra-virgin olive oil
½ large head green cabbage, roughly chopped
1½ cups minced onion
1 large carrot, peeled and finely chopped
1 large celery stalk with leaves, finely chopped
¼ cup tightly packed minced fresh parsley leaves
3 (3-inch) sprigs fresh rosemary, or 2 teaspoons dried
2 tablespoons tightly packed minced
   fresh marjoram leaves, or 1 tablespoon dried
3 cloves garlic, minced
4 or 5 new potatoes, peeled and diced
1 teaspoon salt
½ teaspoon ground black pepper

Slice the sausage thinly and place in a large saucepan along with the chicken broth, pearl barley, and bay leaves. Bring to a boil; reduce the heat and simmer, partially covered, for 30 minutes.

In a large skillet, heat the olive oil over medium heat. Add the cabbage and cook, stirring, until the cabbage begins to wilt, 5 to 10 minutes. Add the onion, carrot, celery, parsley, and rosemary. Cook, stirring often, until the onion is browned, 10 to 15 minutes. Stir in the marjoram and garlic. Add 1 cup liquid from the soup pot and scrape the bottom of the skillet to loosen any browned bits.

Add the cabbage mixture to the soup along with the potatoes. Cover and simmer gently until the barley is tender but not mushy and the potatoes are cooked but firm, about 30 minutes. Remove the bay leaves. Season with salt and pepper. Serve hot.

MAKES 8 TO 10 SERVINGS

MARJORAM

According to Greek mythology, sweet marjoram was first raised by Aphrodite, the goddess of love. It derived its sweet fragrance from her touch. Its scent lingered to remind people of her beauty. In Greece its name means "joy of the mountains."

Marjoram is the symbol of happiness and honor. Garlands of sweet marjoram were worn by happy young couples in ancient Greece and Rome.

Dessert Soups

COLD CHERRY SOUP

This refreshing, unusual summer soup illustrates how well tarragon enhances fruit dishes.

3 cups cold water
½ cup sugar
1 (3-inch) cinnamon stick
4 cups canned sour cherries
1 tablespoon arrowroot
2 tablespoons cold water

¾ teaspoon dried French tarragon, crumbled
½ cup heavy cream, chilled
¾ cup dry red wine, chilled
Borage flowers with seeds and sepals removed for garnish (optional)

In a medium saucepan, combine the water, sugar, and cinnamon. Bring to a boil and add the cherries. Partially cover and simmer over low heat 10 minutes if using canned cherries, 35 to 40 minutes if the cherries are fresh.

Remove the cinnamon stick. Mix the arrowroot and water into a paste; whisk into the cherry soup. Stirring constantly, bring the soup almost to a boil. Reduce the heat, add the tarragon, and simmer 2 minutes more, until clear and slightly thickened. Pour into a shallow bowl; refrigerate until chilled. Before serving in chilled glasses or mugs, stir in the cream and wine. Garnish with a blue borage flower if desired.

✿ VARIATION: *You can use pitted fresh tart cherries instead of canned sour cherries. Increase the sugar to 1 cup. Also, you can vary this with another fruit-enhancing herb, fresh mint, and garnish with a mint leaf.*

MAKES 4 SERVINGS

QUICK COLD CHERRY SOUP WITH SWEET WOODRUFF

Sweet woodruff has a flavor reminiscent of vanilla and complements the slight almond flavor of the cherries.

1 (15-ounce) can pitted dark cherries
¼ teaspoon ground cinnamon
1⅜ cups plain yogurt
½ teaspoon fresh sweet woodruff leaves

½ cup yogurt or sour cream for garnish
Borage flowers with the sepals and seeds
  removed for garnish

Place the cherries, cinnamon, yogurt, and woodruff leaves in a blender. Process several seconds until smooth. Place in the refrigerator. Serve chilled in punch cups or mugs. Garnish with a small dollop of yogurt or sour cream and a borage flower on top.

MAKES 4 SERVINGS

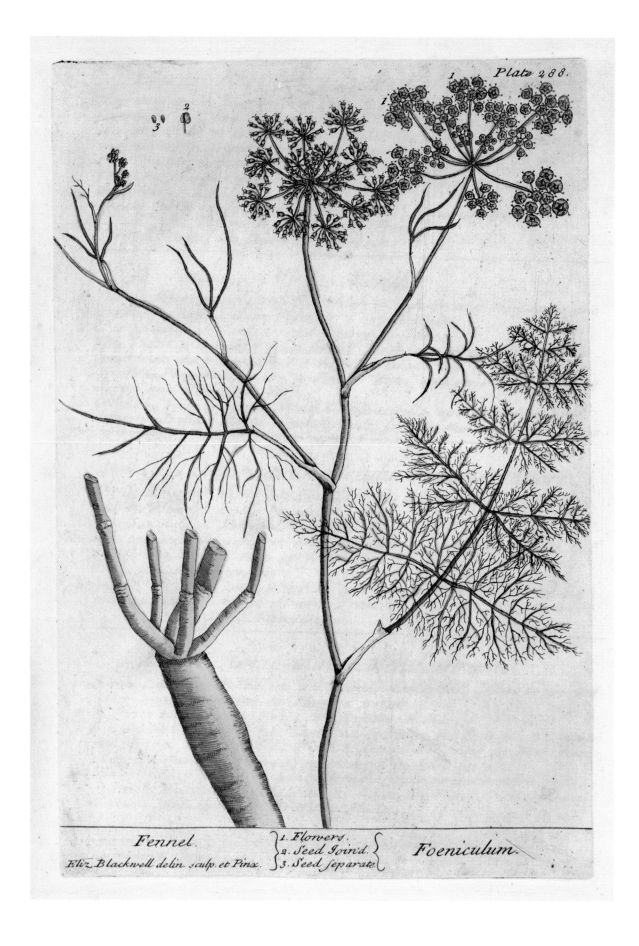

Plate 288.

Fennel.

1. Flowers.
2. Seed Join'd.
3. Seed separate.

Foeniculum.

Eliz. Blackwell delin. sculp. et Pinx.

CHAPTER 6

Breads

If you make your own bread, vary a favorite recipe by adding any of the seed herbs such as fennel, dill, caraway, poppy, nigella, or anise. Rosemary and chives also work well in bread.

ROSEMARY BREAD

Delicious by itself, this hearty bread also makes wonderful lamb sandwiches.

1 package active dry yeast
1 ¾ teaspoons dried rosemary
1 cup warm water
½ teaspoon sugar
1 teaspoon salt

1 cup whole-wheat flour
2 ½ cups unsifted all-purpose flour,
   plus more as needed
Vegetable oil
1 egg yolk, blended with
   1 tablespoon water

ROSEMARY

Seethe the roote in vineger or wine,

and let a thiefe washe his feete

therein, and he shall neither rob,

steale, feare, nor fright any man.

LANGHAM

In a large bowl, sprinkle the yeast and 1 ½ teaspoons of the rosemary over the water; let stand for 5 minutes. Stir in the sugar, salt, whole-wheat flour, and ¾ cup of the all-purpose flour. Using a wooden spoon or a heavy-duty mixer, beat until the mixture pulls away from the bowl in stretchy strands. Gradually beat in 1 ¼ cups of all-purpose flour to form a stiff dough.

Turn the dough out onto a lightly floured surface and knead, adding more flour as necessary, until the dough is smooth and elastic, about 10 minutes. Place the dough in a greased bowl, turning over to grease the top. Cover and let rise in a warm place until doubled in bulk, about 1 hour.

Punch the dough down, turn out onto a floured surface, and knead lightly. Shape into a smooth loaf and place in a greased 4 × 8-inch loaf pan. Brush the top lightly with vegetable oil. Cover with plastic wrap and let rise in a warm place until doubled in bulk, about 1 hour.

Brush the top with the egg yolk mixture, then sprinkle with the remaining rosemary. Bake at 375 degrees until the top is nicely browned and sounds hollow when tapped, about 45 minutes. Turn the bread out of the pan and cool completely on a rack.

MAKES 1 LOAF

HERB PULL-APARTS

A pretty, as well as tasty, bread.

1 cup rye flour
2½ cups unbleached all-purpose flour
1½ teaspoons salt
2 packages active dry yeast
2 tablespoons sugar
½ cup minced onion

1 (12-ounce) can light beer,
  at room temperature
2 tablespoons sesame seeds
2 tablespoons caraway seeds
1 tablespoon poppy seeds
1 ounce Swiss or Gruyère cheese, shredded

Combine the rye flour, all-purpose flour, salt, yeast, sugar, and onion in a food processor. With the machine running, add the beer in a thin stream within 20 seconds; process for another 30 to 40 seconds until the mixture forms a moist, sticky ball. Add additional flour as needed if the dough is too soft.

Rinse a large bowl with hot water but do not dry. Transfer the dough to the bowl and cover tightly with plastic wrap. Set aside until the dough triples in volume, about 2½ hours, depending on the room's temperature.

Turn the dough out onto a generously floured surface. Without kneading, cut the dough into 3 equal pieces. Cut each piece into 5 equal pieces to make a total of 15 small pieces of dough. With floured hands, shape each piece of dough into a smooth ball.

Sprinkle 1 tablespoon sesame seeds evenly in the center of a large baking sheet. Place 1 ball of dough in the center of the baking sheet. Place 5 balls of dough barely touching the first, in a circle around the center.

For the outer ring, you will use the remaining 9 balls of dough. With slightly wet hands, moisten 3 balls and coat both sides generously with the remaining 1 tablespoon sesame seeds. Dip the next 3 balls in caraway seeds, and the final 3 in poppy seeds. Arrange the dough balls in a ring, alternating seed coatings. They should barely touch on the sheet so that the bread will hold together when it rises and bakes. Cover the dough with a dry towel. Set aside until the dough doubles, about 1 to 1½ hours.

Place the oven rack in its lowest position. Sprinkle cheese over the center dough ball and the inner ring. Bake at 350 degrees for 30 minutes, until golden. Cool to room temperature. To serve, pull the bread apart.

MAKES 8 TO 15 SERVINGS

CARAWAY

Of Caruwaies. The Vertues. It consumeth winde,

it is delightful to the stomacke and taste,

it helpeth concoction, provoketh urine, and is

mixed with counter poyson: the root may be

sodden and eaten as the parsenep or carrot is.

GERARD

SWEDISH LIMPA BREAD

Worth making simply for the wonderful aroma that will fill your house!

1 package active dry yeast
1¼ cups water
½ cup cracked wheat
1 teaspoon crushed fennel seeds
1 teaspoon crushed cumin seeds
1½ teaspoons grated orange zest
2 teaspoons salt

⅓ cup molasses
3 tablespoons shortening
1 cup milk, scalded
2 cups unsifted rye flour
4½ cups sifted all-purpose flour
1 tablespoon butter, melted

Dissolve the yeast in ¼ cup warm water; set aside. Combine cracked wheat, fennel, cumin, orange zest, salt, molasses, and shortening, and pour 1 cup boiling water over the mixture. This brewing will tease out the flavor of the seeds. When the mixture cools to lukewarm, add the yeast. Stir in the milk and rye flour. Add enough all-purpose flour to make a moderately stiff dough.

Turn the dough out onto a lightly floured surface and knead for about 10 minutes, until the dough is smooth and elastic. Place in a large oiled bowl. Lightly oil the top of the dough, cover with plastic wrap, and set in a warm place to rise until nearly doubled, about 2 hours. Punch down and form into 1 large (12-inch) or 2 small (9-inch) round loaves. Place on a greased baking sheet. Let rise again until almost doubled in bulk, about 1 hour.

Preheat the oven to 350 degrees. Place the bread on the lower oven shelf. Bake 1 hour 15 minutes for a 12-inch loaf, or 35 minutes for two 9-inch loaves. Remove from the oven, brush the top crusts with melted butter, and cool. Serve, or freeze to store.

MAKES ONE 12-INCH LOAF OR TWO 9-INCH LOAVES

HERBED FOCACCIA

Serve this wonderful summertime bread with a platter of thickly sliced garden tomatoes, alternated with sliced fresh mozzarella cheese, sprinkled with slivers of fresh basil, and drizzled with some olive oil and balsamic vinegar. A simple but delicious meal to eat out of doors!

1 teaspoon dry yeast
½ cup warm water
1½ to 1¾ cups all-purpose flour
1 tablespoon minced fresh oregano,
   or 1 teaspoon dried oregano, crumbled
1 teaspoon salt

4 tablespoons olive oil
1 medium onion, thinly sliced
2 cloves garlic, minced
Salt and freshly ground black pepper to taste
½ cup grated Parmesan cheese

Sprinkle the yeast over water in the bowl of a heavy-duty mixer. (The dough can also be made in a food processor or by hand.) Stir to dissolve. Let the yeast and water stand until foamy, about 5 minutes. Mix in 1 cup flour, oregano, and salt. Mix in enough of the remaining flour to form dough that pulls away from the sides of the bowl.

Turn the dough out onto a lightly floured surface and knead until smooth and elastic, about 5 minutes. Oil a medium bowl. Add the dough, turning over to coat the entire surface. Cover and let rise in a warm, draft-free area until doubled, about 1 hour.

Meanwhile, heat 2 tablespoons oil in a heavy, small skillet over low heat. Add the onion and garlic; cook until the onion and garlic are very tender and golden, stirring occasionally. Season with salt and pepper.

Lightly oil a baking sheet. Punch the dough down. Turn the dough out onto a surface and roll into a ½-inch-thick rectangle. Place on the prepared baking sheet. Using two fingers, make indentations over the surface of the dough. Spread with the onion and garlic. Sprinkle with cheese. Drizzle with the remaining 2 tablespoons olive oil. Let rise in a warm, draft-free area for 30 minutes.

Bake the bread in a 450-degree oven until crisp and golden brown, about 30 minutes. Cut into squares and serve.

MAKES 1 LOAF

ONION THYME BREAD

A versatile bread: punch the dough down thin and it is a cracker;
let it remain 1 inch high and it is an excellent bread to serve with dinner.

Bread

4 teaspoons active dry yeast
¼ teaspoon sugar
½ cup warm water
½ teaspoon coarsely ground
    black pepper
2 teaspoons salt
1 tablespoon olive oil
1 egg
2 cups all-purpose flour

Topping

Olive oil
¼ cup thinly sliced green onion
2 sprigs, plus 1 tablespoon,
    finely chopped fresh thyme,
    or ½ teaspoon dried thyme

Dissolve the yeast and sugar in water. When mixture is bubbly, add the pepper, salt, olive oil, and egg. Stir in 1½ cups flour, then enough more to make a dough. Knead until smooth and no longer sticky, about 10 minutes. Cover and let rise in a warm, draft-free place until doubled, about 1 hour.

Punch the dough down and shape into a flat oval about 1 inch thick. Place on a lightly oiled baking sheet. Make indentations with your finger every 2 inches. Brush lightly with olive oil. Sprinkle the green onion and thyme on top. The thyme sprigs can be placed on top for a fresh look. Cover and let rise in a warm place until puffy, 30 minutes or more.

Preheat oven to 375 degrees. Bake for 20 to 25 minutes, until browned. Cooled bread can be wrapped and frozen to be warmed later.

MAKES 4 TO 6 SERVINGS

DILL COTTAGE CHEESE BREAD

This bread slices or pulls apart easily.

½ cup milk

2 cups cottage cheese

1 tablespoon rapid-rise yeast

1 tablespoon sugar

3 tablespoons minced green onion

2 tablespoons dried dill

4 cups bread flour, plus more as needed

1 egg yolk

1 tablespoon heavy cream

½ teaspoon kosher salt

❧ DILL ❧

Greene Dill, swageth ache,

provoketh sleepe, ripeneth

raw humours. The oyle is good

for wearinesse in Winter,

for it softeneth and moysteneth,

it is good for flegmaticke, agues,

and cold diseases and swellings.

LANGHAM

Scald the milk. In a food processor or large bowl, combine the milk with the cottage cheese. Allow the mixture to cool. Add the yeast, sugar, green onion, dill, and flour. Mix until the dough becomes satiny and elastic. Transfer to a lightly oiled large bowl, turning to coat the dough. Cover with a damp cloth; let rise in a warm, draft-free place until doubled in volume.

Turn the dough out onto a floured surface and divide into 6 equal pieces. Form each piece into a 12-inch-long rope. Braid each set of three pieces, crimping and turning under the ends; place on an oiled baking sheet. Leave enough room for the second loaf so that the loaves can double and not touch. Cover with a damp towel and let the loaves rise for approximately 45 minutes, until a light touch leaves an indentation in the dough.

Preheat the oven to 375 degrees at least 15 minutes before the loaves are ready to bake. Whip the egg yolk with the cream; brush the loaves with the wash. Sprinkle the loaves with kosher salt and bake for 25 to 35 minutes. When you tap the bottom of the loaves, they should sound hollow. Cool on a rack away from drafts. This bread freezes nicely. **MAKES 2 LOAVES**

ROSEMARY FLAT BREAD

A crispy bread perfect with a favorite dip or hot bowl of soup.

1 cup water (105 to 115 degrees)

1 package active dry yeast

1 teaspoon sugar

¼ cup (2 ounces) butter or margarine, melted and cooled

3¼ to 3¾ cups unsifted flour (regular or bread)

1½ teaspoons salt

2 to 3 tablespoons fresh chopped rosemary

Measure warm water into a large, warmed bowl. Sprinkle in the yeast and sugar. Stir until dissolved; let set until bubbly.

Add the melted butter, 2 cups of the flour, salt, and rosemary; beat until smooth. Add enough flour to make a stiff dough. Turn the dough out onto a lightly floured surface and knead until it is smooth and elastic, 8 to 10 minutes. Place in a greased bowl, cover, and let rise in a warm place until doubled, about 1 hour.

Punch the dough down; divide into 4 equal pieces. Roll with a rolling pin and stretch the dough to be the size of a baking sheet. Carefully lift and stretch each piece onto an ungreased baking sheet. If the rosemary makes holes in the dough, just pat it all back together.

Bake at 350 degrees for about 20 minutes, until golden brown. For a more even browning, lift the bread off the baking sheet with a spatula and place on the oven rack for the last few minutes of baking. Cool and break into pieces.

VARIATION: *Before baking the bread, brush beaten egg on the flattened dough and sprinkle the rosemary on top instead of putting it inside the dough. (The flavor is more intense when the herb is inside the bread.) Poppy, sesame, or caraway seeds can also be placed on top after the dough is brushed with beaten egg. Or, instead of rosemary, try making the bread with another favorite herb.*

MAKES 4 LOAVES

ROSEMARY

Because of its association with memory and remembrance, rosemary became an emblem of fidelity for lovers. Brides often wore it as a garland, and wedding guests received a rosemary branch, often gilded and tied with colorful ribbons, as a symbol of love and remembrance. In Wales a sprig of rosemary was cast upon the coffin of a loved one as the coffin was lowered into the ground.

LAVENDER BUTTERMILK LOAVES

Lavender buds are best harvested when just a few flowers begin to open. Cut the spike of flowers, rinse quickly, and pat dry, then set the stems in a single layer on a paper towel in a basket to dry. Remove the buds when they are dry. Store in a small glass jar until ready to use.

3 ¾ teaspoons rapid-rise yeast
1 cup lukewarm water
1 cup buttermilk
⅓ cup olive oil
¼ cup fresh or dried English lavender flowers, finely chopped

1 tablespoon regular salt
½ cup semolina
4½ to 6 cups unbleached all-purpose flour
Cornmeal for dusting
Sprinkle of coarse salt

In the food processor, stir the yeast into water. Let stand until the mixture is foamy, about 10 minutes. Add the buttermilk, oil, lavender, and regular salt; mix until everything is well blended. Add the semolina and flour gradually, beating until incorporated.

Turn the dough out onto a floured surface. Knead by hand until the dough is smooth and elastic, about 2 minutes. Put the dough in an oiled bowl, turning to coat with oil. Cover with plastic wrap and let rise in a warm place until doubled in bulk, about 1½ hours.

Oil a baking sheet and dust with cornmeal. Turn the dough out onto a floured surface and divide it in half. Shape each half into a round and put the halves on the prepared baking sheet. Cover them with plastic wrap and let rise 1 hour.

Heat oven to 425 degrees. With a sharp knife, gently slash the top of each loaf in the shape of a large asterisk; sprinkle with coarse salt. Bake in the middle of the oven, spraying the loaves occasionally with water during the first 15 minutes. Bake 30 minutes more, until the loaves sound hollow when tapped on the bottom. Transfer to a rack and cool.

MAKES 2 LOAVES

LAVENDER

According to Mrs. M. Grieve in A Modern Herbal *(1931), lavender was used in earlier days as a condiment and for flavoring dishes "to comfort the stomach." She continues, "It is agreeable to the taste and smell, provokes appetite, raises the spirits and dispels flatulence."*

Quick Breads

CARAWAY ANISE SWEET BREAD

A welcome change from the standard tea breads.

3 cups sifted all-purpose flour
4 teaspoons baking powder
½ teaspoon salt
⅓ cup butter or margarine
1 cup sugar

2 eggs
1¼ cups milk
1 tablespoon caraway seeds
½ teaspoon anise seeds
1 teaspoon vanilla

Sift the flour, baking powder, and salt together; set aside. Cream the butter and sugar in a large bowl until fluffy. Add the eggs and beat until light. Alternately blend in the flour mixture and the milk, about a third at a time, until well blended. Add the caraway and anise seeds and vanilla.

Pour the batter into a well-greased 9 × 5-inch loaf pan. Bake in a 350-degree oven 1 to 1¼ hours, until a toothpick inserted into the center comes out clean. Cool on a rack 10 minutes; remove from the pan. Let loaf cool on the rack.

MAKES 1 LOAF

> ### CARAWAY
>
> *The seeds confected, or made with sugar into comfits, are very good for the stomacke, they helpe digestion, provoke urine, assuage and dissolve all windenesse: to conclude in a word, they are answerable to Anise seed in opertions and vertues.* GERARD

IRISH SODA BREAD

Delightful when toasted and served with cream cheese, this bread is based on a soda bread recipe from Ireland written down in the 1890s.

4 cups all-purpose flour
4 teaspoons baking powder
½ teaspoon baking soda
1 teaspoon salt

3 tablespoons sugar
2 tablespoons caraway seeds
1 cup dark seedless raisins (or more)
2 cups buttermilk

Preheat the oven to 350 degrees. Combine the flour, baking powder, baking soda, salt, sugar, caraway seeds, and raisins. Add the buttermilk. Mix until it forms a soft dough. Turn the dough out onto a floured surface and knead a few times, using extra flour as needed. Lightly form it into a round loaf and put into a greased 12-inch cast-iron skillet or on a baking sheet. Bake until the crust is golden brown, 50 minutes to 1 hour 15 minutes.

MAKES 1 LOAF

Plate 374.

1

2 3

Anise.

Eliz. Blackwell delin. sculp. et Pinx.

} 1. *Flower.*
2. *Seed.*
3. *Seed separate.* {

Anisum.

Biscuits, Muffins, and Scones

HERB POPOVERS

A variation on plain popovers.

1 cup all-purpose flour
1 cup milk
2 large eggs
1 tablespoon vegetable oil
½ teaspoon salt
3 tablespoons minced parsley

1 green onion, minced
1 teaspoon fresh thyme,
    or ½ teaspoon dried
1 teaspoon fresh sage,
    or ½ teaspoon dried

Lightly coat 12 muffin cups with cooking spray.

Put the flour, milk, eggs, oil, and salt in a blender. Pulse until the mixture is well blended, scraping down the sides 2 or 3 times. Stir in the parsley, green onion, thyme, and sage. Pour the batter equally into muffin cups.

Bake the popovers 30 to 35 minutes in a 425-degree oven until they are puffed and well browned. Unmold onto a rack. Pierce each popover with a small knife to release the steam. Serve immediately.

MAKES 12 POPOVERS

PARSLEY

An old English adage claimed,

"Fried parsley will bring

a man to his saddle

and a woman to her grave."

BUTTERMILK HERB BISCUITS

Use leftover biscuits—if there are any—for sandwiches.

2 cups all-purpose flour
2½ teaspoons baking powder
½ teaspoon salt
½ teaspoon dry mustard
¼ teaspoon baking soda
½ cup shortening

3 tablespoons minced fresh parsley
½ teaspoon minced fresh thyme,
  or ¼ teaspoon dried thyme, crushed
1 tablespoon minced fresh chives
  or green onion
⅔ cup buttermilk or sour milk

Combine the flour, baking powder, salt, dry mustard, and soda in a large bowl. Cut in the shortening until the mixture looks like cornmeal. Stir in the parsley, thyme, and chives. Make a well in the center and pour in the buttermilk. Stir the dough with a fork, just enough to form it into a ball. The dough will be very soft.

Turn the dough out onto a lightly floured surface and knead it gently 15 times, adding a minimum of additional flour. Roll or pat out the dough into a ¾-inch-thick rectangle. Cut into 12 pieces with a floured knife or a biscuit cutter. Place pieces ½ inch apart on an ungreased baking sheet.

Bake at 450 degrees for 12 to 15 minutes, until golden brown. Serve hot.

NOTE: *To sour milk, place 2 teaspoons vinegar or lemon juice in a 1-cup liquid measuring cup. Add sweet milk until ⅔ full; let stand for 5 minutes.*

MAKES 12 BISCUITS

WEYKE BRAYNES

William Turner wrote that parsley seed taken before a drinking bout "helpeth men that have weyke braynes to bear drinke better."

SAFFRON SCONES

Serve these scones for breakfast on the weekend or at an afternoon tea.

½ teaspoon lightly packed saffron threads
½ cup buttermilk
2 large eggs
¾ cup (6 ounces) butter
2 cups all-purpose flour

½ cup sugar
2 teaspoons baking powder
1 teaspoon baking soda
¼ teaspoon salt
⅓ cup dried cherries

Crush the saffron threads to a fine powder and add the buttermilk and eggs. Whisk until blended. Set aside. Melt 4 tablespoons of the butter. Set aside to cool.

Combine the flour, sugar, baking powder, baking soda, and salt in a large bowl. Cut in the rest of the butter until the mixture resembles coarse meal. Stir in the dried cherries. Add the saffron-buttermilk mixture. Stir until a soft, sticky dough forms. (This can be placed in a covered container and refrigerated for a few days, or frozen for later use. Return to room temperature before continuing.)

On a well-floured surface, knead the dough once or twice very lightly. Roll the dough into an 8-inch square, about ½ inch thick. Cut into 4 squares. Cut each small square into 4 triangles, 16 triangles total. Place the triangles on a baking sheet about 1 inch apart. Brush lightly with the melted butter.

Bake the scones in the upper-middle rack of a 350-degree oven for 12 to 15 minutes, until lightly browned and firm to the touch. Serve warm or at room temperature. Store in an airtight container for up to a week, or freeze for up to 2 months.

SAFFRON

In both India and Greece, saffron was considered a powerful aphrodisiac. The Arabian Nights declared it was so powerful in this regard it could cause women to swoon with passion and was one of two things that could "corrupt women," the other being gold.

MAKES 16 SCONES

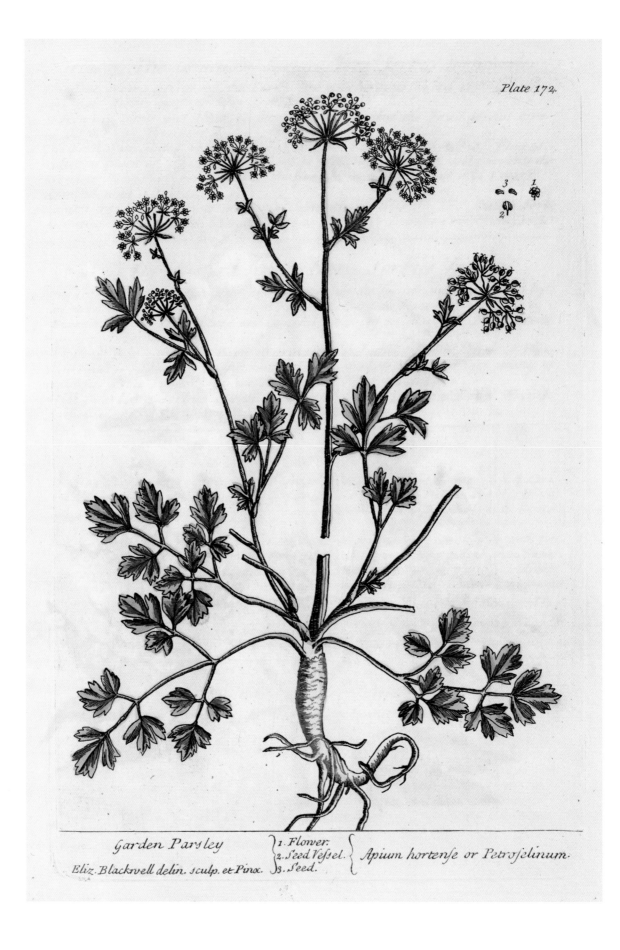

Plate 172.

Garden Parsley

Eliz. Blackwell delin. sculp. et Pinx.

{ 1. Flower.
{ 2. Seed Vessel. } *Apium hortense or Petroselinum.*
{ 3. Seed.

CHAPTER 7

Pasta and Pizza

$\mathcal{I}$f simplicity is the soul of elegance, then pasta qualifies as an elegant food since it has just two basic ingredients, flour and water, or alternatively, flour and eggs. Although ready-made pasta is widely available, a special pleasure lies in making your own, and best of all, you can flavor it with herbs. For additional flavor or color, you might add spinach, red peppers, or lemon zest.

Pasta is surprisingly easy to prepare and can be done in 30 to 40 minutes, but allow an hour if you are preparing a simple sauce to go with it. Use unbleached all-purpose flour if possible, and you may want to get a pasta machine that will roll the dough to the desired thickness.

Recipes for homemade pasta abound; try several until you find your favorite.

Pasta

PASTA WITH OLIVE OIL AND FRESH HERBS

Simple and quick, perfect for a busy day. Or, use this as a side dish with grilled fish, steaks, or chops.

½ cup minced fresh basil
½ cup minced fresh flat-leaf parsley
1 tablespoon minced fresh oregano
1 tablespoon minced fresh thyme
¼ cup extra-virgin olive oil

Salt and pepper to taste
1 clove garlic, minced (optional)
1 anchovy fillet (or to taste),
  minced (optional)
1 pound spaghetti or linguine
Parmesan cheese, toasted pine nuts, slivered
  kalamata olives, or red pepper flakes
  for garnish (optional)

Combine basil, parsley, oregano, and thyme in a large bowl with the olive oil, salt, and pepper. Add the garlic and anchovy, if desired.

Cook the pasta in boiling salted water until al dente; drain and toss with the herbs. Correct the seasoning as necessary and serve. Garnish with Parmesan cheese, pine nuts, olives, or red pepper flakes, if desired.

NOTE: *Use your best olive oil.*

MAKES 4 SERVINGS

> ### ❧ OREGANO ❧
>
> *Fresh Oregano is a stimulative tonic which cures a man's body of choler, consumption of the lungs, the cough, dropsy, infirmities of the spleen, itch, a loss of appetite, scabs, scurvy, and yellow jaundice.* CULPEPER

ARUGULA PASTA

Arugula is easy to grow because it reseeds readily. If you have room for a patch of ground that is 3 to 4 feet square, you can have a constant supply of arugula. Arugula cooks up like spinach but has its own special flavor, and the coarsely chopped bread crumbs in this recipe absorb the garlic/oil flavors, adding an interesting texture.

8 ounces pasta
1 tablespoon butter
7 cloves garlic, minced
¼ cup virgin olive oil

4 cups coarsely chopped arugula
¼ cup dry bread crumbs, preferably
  coarsely chopped, dry, leftover bread
Coarsely ground black pepper to taste

Cook the pasta in 3 quarts of boiling water until al dente. Reserve ¼ cup of the pasta water. Drain the pasta and place in a warmed serving dish. Stir in the butter. Cover and set aside.

Cook the garlic in the oil in the same pan until golden. Add the arugula and stir until wilted. Stir in the bread crumbs, the reserved pasta water, and the pasta until thoroughly combined.

Return to the serving dish. Sprinkle with pepper and serve immediately.

MAKES 4 SERVINGS

PASTA WITH SAFFRON SAUCE

Decadent and fancy, this pasta dresses up any occasion.

2 shallots, finely minced
2 to 3 cloves garlic, finely minced
1 tablespoon olive oil or butter
1 pinch saffron threads or powder
3 tablespoons hot water
¼ cup dry white wine
1 cup heavy cream
1 medium sweet red pepper,
   roasted, peeled, and julienned

1 medium sweet yellow pepper,
   roasted, peeled, and julienned
Salt and white pepper to taste
2 cups shaped pasta such as penne
   or farfalle, cooked and drained
Shavings of white truffle
   for garnish or a few drops
   white truffle oil (optional)

Sauté the shallots, then the garlic, over low heat in the olive oil or butter. Meanwhile, soak the saffron threads or powder in the water. When the shallots and garlic are soft, but not browned, add the wine and raise the heat to medium-high. Reduce the wine until almost evaporated, about 2 tablespoons.

Gradually whisk in the cream so that it will emulsify with the sauce. Cook the sauce until thickened. Add the bell peppers; stir to heat through. Strain the saffron mixture into the sauce. Season to taste with salt and white pepper.

Toss the pasta with the sauce. Add a little of the pasta water if the sauce appears to be too thick. Place the pasta in a serving dish and garnish with shavings of white truffle or white truffle oil, if desired.

VARIATION: Seafood can be used in this dish. Add lobster, scallops, shrimp, or another shellfish right after adding the peppers. Cook for a few minutes prior to adding the saffron mixture.

MAKES 2 SERVINGS

SAFFRON

Saffron is endowed with great virtues, for it refreshes the spirits, and is good against fainting-fits and the palpitation of the heart; it strengthens the stomach, helps digestion, cleanses the lungs, and is good in coughs.

CULPEPER

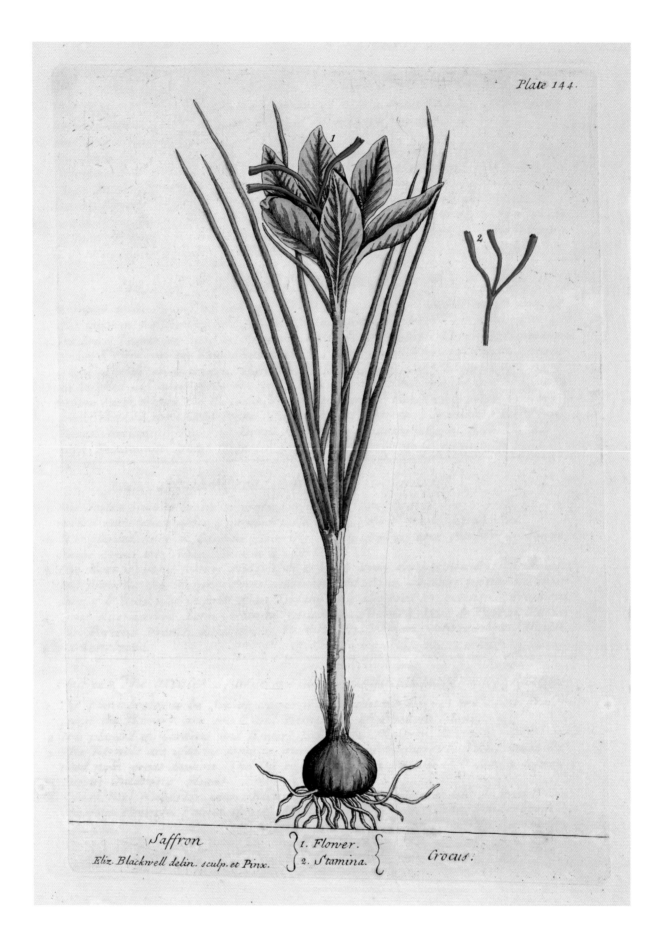

Plate 144.

Saffron

Eliz. Blackwell delin. sculp. et Pinx.

1. Flower.
2. Stamina.

Crocus.

CREAMY FETTUCCINE WITH PROSCIUTTO AND FRESH BASIL

Garnish with whole basil leaves and lots of freshly ground black pepper for a profound, smooth flavor.

¼ cup olive oil
1 pound onions, julienned
3 pounds tomatoes, peeled, seeded, and diced
1 pound prosciutto, julienned
8 cloves garlic, crushed
3 cups heavy cream or half-and-half

¼ cup chopped fresh oregano
¼ cup chopped fresh basil
3½ pounds fresh egg fettuccine
Whole basil leaves for garnish
Freshly ground black pepper for garnish

In a skillet, heat the oil and cook the onion and tomatoes until the onion is soft and translucent. Add the prosciutto and garlic and cook lightly for 2 to 3 minutes. Add the cream, oregano, and basil. Simmer for 30 minutes.

In a large pot of salted boiling water, cook the fettuccine until just al dente, about 2 minutes. Drain the pasta and place it in a warmed serving bowl. Pour the sauce over the hot pasta and serve, garnished with whole basil leaves and black pepper.

MAKES 8 TO 10 SERVINGS

SMOKED SALMON FETTUCCINE

The fresh dill with lemon adds a nice "zest" to this easy-to-make dish. The tomato-less sauce is very creamy and smoky.

2 tablespoons minced fresh dill
Zest of 1 lemon, grated
½ cup capers
¼ cup minced shallots
8 ounces smoked salmon
8 ounces fettuccine, cooked

¼ cup olive oil
2 teaspoons Dijon mustard
Salt and pepper to taste
½ to ¾ cup half-and-half, warmed
4 ounces sliced mushrooms, cooked (optional)

Combine the dill, lemon zest, capers, shallots, and salmon in a bowl. In a separate bowl, combine the cooked fettuccine, olive oil, and mustard and toss gently.

Combine the pasta and salmon mixtures. Add salt and pepper, then the warmed half-and-half. Add the mushrooms, if desired.

MAKES 4 SERVINGS

CAPERS

The Capers preserved in salt or pickel, as they be brought into this countrie, being washed, boyled, and eaten with vineger, are meate and medicine: for it stirreth up appetite, openeth the stoppings of the liver and milt, consumeth and wasteth the colde flemes that is gathered about the stomacke. Yet they nourish very little or not at all, as Galen sayeth. DODOENS

PESTO PASTA WITH SCALLOPS

A refreshing summertime dish.

Pesto

1 cup packed fresh basil

3 cloves garlic, crushed

½ teaspoon salt (optional)

1 to 2 tablespoons pine nuts
  or chopped walnuts

¼ cup olive oil

½ cup grated Parmesan cheese

Scallops

¼ cup dry white wine

2 tablespoons lemon juice

Salt (optional)

Fresh ground black pepper to taste

1 pound bay scallops

1 pound capellini

> ### ❧ GARLIC ❧
>
> *Garlic probably originated in Asia, though early on*
>
> *it spread to the Mediterranean countries. Ancient*
>
> *Egyptians and Romans regarded garlic as both food*
>
> *and medicine, and Egyptians fed it to the slaves who*
>
> *built the pyramids. After the Exodus, the Israelites*
>
> *remembered with longing the garlic they had before they*
>
> *embarked on their great journey through the desert.*

In a blender or food processor, combine the basil, garlic, salt, and nuts. With the motor running, gradually add the oil, blending the mixture until it becomes a smooth paste. Add the Parmesan cheese; process the mixture a few seconds longer to combine thoroughly. Transfer the pesto to a large bowl.

In a medium saucepan, bring the wine, lemon juice, salt, and pepper to a boil; add the scallops. Cook the scallops 2 or 3 minutes, stirring gently. Drain, reserving the liquid.

In a large pot of boiling salted water, cook the capellini until al dente, 2 to 3 minutes. Drain the pasta, add it to the pesto, tossing to coat with the sauce. Gradually add the reserved scallop cooking liquid, tossing to mix. Add the scallops. Refrigerate mixture 1 hour, or as long as overnight.

MAKES 6 SERVINGS

PASTA SHELLS WITH HERBS

Whip up this simple dish in just as much time as it takes to cook the pasta.

2 tablespoons butter

⅓ cup olive oil

4 cloves garlic, minced

½ teaspoon red pepper flakes, or to taste

1 cup chopped fresh flat-leaf parsley

¾ cup minced fresh basil leaves

2 tablespoons minced fresh mint leaves

1 tablespoon minced fresh rosemary

Salt and pepper to taste

1 pound pasta shells

Freshly grated Parmesan cheese to taste

Heat the butter, oil, garlic, and red pepper flakes gently in a large skillet. Add the parsley, basil, mint, and rosemary and cook over low heat for a few minutes. Season with salt and pepper to taste.

Meanwhile, cook the pasta in boiling water until it is not quite al dente because it will cook further in the skillet. Drain well; stir the pasta into the herbs and cook over medium heat until the pasta is well coated.

Sprinkle with Parmesan cheese, mix again, and serve immediately with extra cheese on the side.

MAKES 4 SERVINGS

ORRECHIETTE WITH ROASTED VEGETABLES

If you can't find orrechiette, substitute bowtie pasta in this recipe.

1 zucchini	4 cloves garlic, minced
1 yellow squash	½ teaspoon minced fresh rosemary
1 small eggplant	1 teaspoon minced fresh thyme
½ bulb fresh fennel	1 teaspoon minced fresh oregano
½ red bell pepper	1½ cups chicken broth
½ yellow bell pepper	⅓ cup grated Parmesan cheese
3 tablespoons extra-virgin olive oil	12 ounces orrechiette pasta
Salt and pepper to taste	8 fresh basil leaves, julienned

Preheat the oven to 425 degrees. Cut the zucchini, squash, eggplant, fennel, and bell peppers into ¼-inch pieces; transfer to a large bowl. Toss with 1 tablespoon of the olive oil and a pinch of salt and pepper. Lay out evenly on a baking sheet. Roast for 30 minutes, until tender. Remove from the oven.

In a large pot, heat 1 tablespoon of the olive oil. Add the garlic and cook just until golden. Add the roasted vegetables and rosemary, thyme, and oregano. Toss together, then add the chicken broth. Bring to a boil and simmer 5 minutes. Stir in the remaining 1 tablespoon olive oil and the Parmesan cheese.

In a separate pot, cook the pasta in salted water about 8 minutes, until al dente. Drain.

Toss the pasta and sauce together until well combined. Serve in bowls and top with julienned fresh basil and additional Parmesan cheese, if desired.

MAKES 6 SERVINGS

✦ TO BE SLENDER ✦

Slender to be, eat two or three cloues of Garlick,

with as much Bread and Butter, morne and

euen three houres before and after meat,

and drinke water wherein Fennill hath been

sodden, morne and euen fourteene dayes.

LANGHAM

PASTA AND PIZZA 101

PENNE WITH SAUSAGE AND HERBS

The sausage-herb tomato sauce is great for lasagna.

1 (28-ounce) can artichoke hearts
1 clove garlic, minced
¼ cup olive oil
4 tablespoons butter
1 pound Italian sweet sausage,
   casings removed and discarded
½ tablespoon minced fresh parsley
2 to 3 fresh basil leaves, chopped

2 to 3 fresh oregano leaves, chopped
½ teaspoon red pepper flakes
2 tablespoons dry red wine
1 (28-ounce) can diced tomatoes
Salt and pepper to taste
1 pound penne
½ cup grated pecorino cheese
½ cup grated Parmesan cheese

Drain the artichoke hearts and cut them in half. Place in a dish and salt lightly. Let sit 30 minutes at room temperature.

Sauté the garlic in the oil and 2 tablespoons of the butter in a large saucepan over medium heat. Add the sausage in small chunks. Stirring constantly, cook over medium heat until the sausage begins to brown. Add the parsley, basil, oregano, and red pepper flakes. Cook 5 minutes. Add the wine and stir to evaporate. Add the tomatoes, salt, and pepper; cook 20 minutes. Set aside.

Preheat the oven to 350 degrees. Cook the penne in 8 cups boiling salted water for 10 minutes; drain. Melt the remaining 2 tablespoons butter in a baking dish and add some of the tomato sauce. Combine with the penne, away from the heat. Sprinkle with the pecorino cheese while slowly adding more sauce; add half of the Parmesan cheese. Layer the dish with artichoke hearts. Pour the remaining sauce over it and cover with the rest of the cheese. Bake 10 minutes.

MAKES 6 TO 8 SERVINGS

PARSLEY AND RUE

An early custom was to border the herb garden with parsley and rue. When a project was discussed but not begun, the expression of being "only at the parsley and rue" referred to this stage.

GOAT CHEESE AND BASIL RAVIOLI

Using packaged wonton wrappers reduces the preparation time for these elegant ravioli.

Sauce

- 4 cloves garlic, finely minced
- 2 tablespoons olive oil
- 6 plum tomatoes (2 pounds), peeled, seeded, and coarsely chopped, or 1 (28-ounce) can plum tomatoes, drained and chopped
- 1½ teaspoons minced fresh thyme

Filling

- 12 ounces mild goat cheese, at room temperature
- ¼ cup ricotta cheese
- ¼ cup chopped fresh basil
- 1 large egg

- 1 package wonton wrappers
- Freshly grated Parmesan cheese to taste
- Sprig of fresh basil for garnish

To make the sauce, cook the garlic in oil in a medium saucepan over medium heat for 3 minutes. Stir in the tomatoes and thyme. Reduce the heat to medium-low. Cover and cook for 20 to 30 minutes. (The sauce can be made ahead and reheated.)

To make the filling, place the goat cheese, ricotta cheese, basil, and egg in a food processor; process until smooth.

Place 1 tablespoon of the filling in the center of a wonton wrapper. Moisten the edges of the wrapper with water. Place another wrapper over the filling and press down to remove the air. Press the edges to seal. The edges can be decoratively trimmed.

Repeat the process until all of the filling is used. To keep the filled ravioli pliable, place them on a dry kitchen towel as they are made, and cover with plastic wrap.

Bring 6 quarts of water to a boil in a large pot. Reduce the heat to a gentle boil. Add the ravioli and cook 3 to 5 minutes. Do not overcook. Transfer the ravioli with a slotted spoon to a warm platter. Spoon the sauce over the ravioli. Sprinkle with Parmesan cheese and garnish with a sprig of fresh basil.

MAKES 6 SERVINGS

BASIL

. . . being gently handled it gave a pleasant smell, but being gardly wrung and bruised would breed scorpions. It is also observed that scorpions doe much rest and abide under these pots and vessells wherein Basil is planted.

PARKINSON

PUMPKIN RAVIOLI WITH SAGE BUTTER SAUCE

A little bit extra work, but well worth it. If you enjoy making your own bread, you will love making your own ravioli.

Pasta

2¼ cups all-purpose flour

3 eggs

Pinch of salt

1 beaten egg to wet and seal the ravioli

Filling

1 cup cooked fresh pumpkin
   or canned pumpkin

½ cup ricotta cheese

6 amaretti cookies, crushed

¾ teaspoon salt, or to taste

¼ teaspoon white pepper, or to taste

¼ teaspoon ground nutmeg

⅛ teaspoon ground cinnamon

¼ teaspoon anise seed

⅛ teaspoon ground thyme

1 egg, beaten

Sauce

4 tablespoons butter

8 fresh sage leaves

1½ to 2 cups whipping cream

3 tablespoons freshly grated
   Parmesan cheese

Additional fresh sage leaves,
   slivered, for garnish

To make the pasta dough, mix the flour, 3 eggs, and salt with a fork. Add a tiny bit more flour if too wet or a tiny bit of water if too stiff. It should feel like pie dough. On a lightly floured board, knead the dough a minute or two until it feels smooth. Place in a plastic bag and set aside for 30 minutes.

Pinch off a piece of dough about the size of a large egg. Following the directions for your pasta machine, roll the dough between successively closer rollers until about ⅛ to 1/16 inch thick. Or roll to that thickness with a rolling pin until you have a strip about 4 inches wide. Lay each strip on a flat surface covered with a lightly floured towel. Sprinkle lightly with flour. Continue rolling out all of the strips in the same manner.

Make the filling by combining the cooked pumpkin, ricotta cheese, amaretti, salt, pepper, nutmeg, cinnamon, anise, thyme, and egg.

Brush the pasta dough with the beaten egg. Spoon about 2 teaspoons at a time of the filling onto the pasta, leaving about 3 inches of space between dollops. (Use just enough filling to make nice, bite-sized portions; don't overfill or the filling might ooze out.) Cover with a second sheet of ravioli. Press pasta down along edges to seal.

Cut with a ravioli cutter, a knife, or a glass that is not more than 2½ inches in diameter. Pinch all edges together. Lay ravioli in a single layer on a lightly floured cloth. Sprinkle tops lightly with flour. Allow to dry about 2 hours, turning ravioli once and sprinkling again lightly with flour. Ravioli can then be placed between layers of parchment paper in a plastic freezer container and frozen for up to 2 weeks.

To cook the ravioli, bring a large quantity of water to a full boil. Add 1 tablespoon salt. If frozen, simmer ravioli 5 to 6 minutes. If fresh, simmer for 2 to 3 minutes, until al dente. Drain in a large colander.

To make the sauce, melt the butter in a large saucepan over low heat. Add the sage and cream and bring to a simmer. Simmer 1 minute.

To serve, place the drained ravioli on a large platter. Pour the sage butter sauce over the ravioli. Sprinkle with Parmesan cheese. Garnish with slivered fresh sage leaves. Serve immediately.

Variation: If you do not have time to make the ravioli dough from scratch, you can substitute wonton wrappers. Be sure to seal the edges well with a paste of cornstarch and water.

MAKES ABOUT 20 TO 25 RAVIOLI, OR 4 SERVINGS

BAKED PASTA WITH SPINACH, GOAT CHEESE, AND TOMATOES

This pasta can be assembled a day ahead of time; just refrigerate and bring to room temperature before baking.

8 ounces radiatore or fusilli pasta

5 tablespoons light olive oil

2 (14½-ounce) cans chunky-style stewed tomatoes

¼ teaspoon red pepper flakes

2 (10-ounce) packages frozen whole-leaf spinach, thawed, or 2 bunches fresh

3 cloves garlic

1 medium shallot

1 large egg

1 cup ricotta cheese

½ teaspoon salt

½ teaspoon ground nutmeg

¼ teaspoon black pepper

½ teaspoon minced fresh or dried rosemary

1 tablespoon minced fresh basil, or 1 teaspoon dried

1 teaspoon minced fresh oregano, or ½ teaspoon dried

7 ounces soft goat cheese

Cook the pasta, drain, and toss with 1 tablespoon of the olive oil. Drain the tomatoes, reserving 3 tablespoons of the liquid. Toss the tomatoes with 2 tablespoons of the olive oil and the red pepper flakes.

Wrap the spinach in a cloth towel and wring out the moisture. Mince the garlic and shallot in a food processor. Add the spinach, egg, ricotta, salt, nutmeg, and pepper. Process until just combined. Spread evenly in a lightly oiled, shallow, 2-quart baking dish.

Spread the pasta in an even layer over the spinach. Drizzle the reserved tomato liquid over the pasta, then add the tomatoes.

Combine 1 tablespoon olive oil, rosemary, basil, and oregano in a small bowl. Cut the goat cheese into ½-inch chunks. Toss lightly in the herb-oil mixture. Arrange over the pasta to cover. Drizzle with 1 tablespoon olive oil and sprinkle lightly with salt.

Preheat the oven to 375 degrees. Loosely tent the dish with foil and place on a baking sheet. Place in the middle of the oven and bake for 1 hour 10 minutes. Remove the foil and bake uncovered for 10 minutes more. Serve hot.

MAKES 4 TO 6 SERVINGS

Plate 319.

Sweet Marjoram.

Eliz. Blackwell delin. sculp. et Pinx.

1. *Flower.*
2. *Cup.*
3. *Seed.*

Majorana.

CHAPTER 8

Vegetables and Side Dishes

Gardeners graze and nibble on cherry tomatoes, peas, carrots, strawberries, and even sweet corn while working and weeding in the garden. When we can't forage, we enjoy cooking and embellishing vegetables. Celebrate their ripeness by picking the freshest ones, cooking—but not overcooking—them, seasoning them lightly with herb butters, and serving them in a simple fashion. To bring out the bright color of green vegetables, do not cover while cooking or add vinegar or lemon juice.

BROCCOLI WITH
LEMON GRASS AND HERBS

With a subtle lemon flavor of the Pacific Rim, this dish can be as mild or spicy as you like.

2 tablespoons virgin olive oil
2 cloves garlic, minced
1 small onion, sliced
1 tablespoon minced lemon grass
  (tender white core only)
1 tablespoon minced fresh ginger
1 Roma tomato, seeded and coarsely chopped
  (about ¼ cup)
1 jalapeño pepper, seeded
  and thinly sliced

1 pound fresh broccoli
  (florets and coarsely chopped stems)
½ cup julienned red bell pepper
½ cup julienned yellow bell pepper
8 ounces fresh mushrooms, sliced
1 teaspoon minced fresh cilantro
1 cup sliced fresh basil
⅛ teaspoon red pepper flakes (optional)
Salt to taste

Heat the oil in a large skillet or wok. Add the garlic, onion, lemon grass, ginger, tomato, and jalapeño. Stir-fry for a few minutes to release the flavors.

Add the broccoli; stir-fry 5 minutes, until the color changes to bright green. Add the red and yellow peppers, mushrooms, cilantro, and basil. Stir-fry 5 more minutes. Add the red pepper flakes and salt to taste.

MAKES 6 TO 8 SERVINGS

CAULIFLOWER IN
SPICY TOMATO CURRY

1 tablespoon coriander seeds
1 ½ teaspoons cumin seeds
¼ teaspoon anise or fennel seeds
1 tablespoon peanut oil
1 cup chopped onion
1 clove garlic, minced
1 tablespoon julienned fresh ginger
1 teaspoon sugar

½ teaspoon turmeric
¼ teaspoon cayenne
1 ½ cups tomato juice
2 to 2 ½ pounds cauliflower, trimmed
Coarse salt to taste
⅓ cup unsalted roasted peanuts, chopped
¼ to ½ cup minced fresh
  cilantro or parsley

In a spice grinder, finely grind the coriander, cumin, and anise seeds. In a heavy pot or Dutch oven, heat the oil over medium heat. Add the onion and garlic; sauté to soften, about 3 minutes. Add the ginger, sugar, turmeric, cayenne, and the ground spice mixture. Stir for 1 minute. Add the tomato juice and bring to a simmer. Cover and cook over low heat, stirring occasionally, for 5 minutes.

Add the cauliflower and stir to coat with the sauce. Cover and simmer, stirring occasionally, until the cauliflower is soft, about 10 to 15 minutes. Season with salt. Transfer to a serving dish; sprinkle with peanuts and cilantro or parsley. Serve with white rice.

🌿 VARIATION : *If you like your curry extra-spicy, add ¼ to ½ teaspoon extra cayenne to the ground spice mixture.*

MAKES 4 TO 6 SERVINGS

CORIANDER

Coriander seed has many uses and is known as a mainstay in flavoring pickles, gin, corned beef, sausages, bread, and cookies. Try some crushed seed in pea soup or poultry stuffing. Like many of the other seed herbs, it works well with fruit pies and tarts for a lovely variation.

ONIONS ESCOFFIER

From simple ingredients comes a fine dish that reflects the heritage of French cookery.

1 ¾ pounds small white onions
2 tablespoons vegetable oil
Salt and pepper to taste
1 bay leaf
Pinch of dried thyme

1 teaspoon fennel seeds
3 tablespoons golden raisins, soaked in
    lukewarm water until plump
½ cup dry white wine
¼ cup cognac

FENNEL

Fenell provoketh men to the procreation of childer. The serpents chew this herb and purge and clear their eyes therewith, whereof learned men did gather that it should also be good for man's eyes.

TURNER

Peel the onions and boil 5 minutes. Drain and pat dry. Heat the oil in a large skillet; add the onions, season with salt and pepper, and fry gently until golden brown, being careful not to let them burn.

Add the bay leaf, thyme, fennel seeds, and golden raisins; pour in the wine and cognac. Bring to a boil, cover, and cook 5 minutes. Remove from heat, allow to cool, remove the bay leaf, and serve.

MAKES 4 SERVINGS

STUFFED ARTICHOKES

A nice change from plain boiled artichokes.

3 large artichokes
1 2 ounces sliced bacon (optional)
5 cups Italian bread crumbs
¾ cup grated Romano cheese
¾ cup grated Parmesan cheese
¼ cup minced fresh chives
¼ cup minced fresh parsley
½ cup chopped green onion

4 cloves garlic, minced
1 tablespoon salt
1 ½ tablespoons minced fresh oregano
1 ½ tablespoons minced fresh basil
1 teaspoon cayenne
½ tablespoon freshly ground black pepper
¾ cup olive oil (¼ cup per artichoke)
3 lemon slices

Prepare the artichokes for steaming. Fry the bacon until crisp. Crumble the bacon in a bowl; add the bread crumbs, cheese, chives, parsley, green onion, garlic, salt, oregano, basil, cayenne, and black pepper. Spread out the artichoke leaves and pack with the stuffing.

Set the artichokes in a roasting pan filled with 1 ½ inches of water. Pour ¼ cup olive oil over each artichoke. Top each with a slice of lemon. Bring water to a boil, cover, and simmer 1 hour.

SERVES 3

WHITE BEANS WITH SPINACH, SAGE, AND THYME

Easy to prepare, this dish is excellent at a barbecue or beach party.

1 pound small dried white beans, soaked in
    water overnight and drained
2 cups chicken broth
2 cups beef broth
⅔ cup chopped onion
6 cloves garlic, chopped

1 jalapeño pepper, seeded and finely minced
6 to 1 0 sprigs fresh thyme, leaves only
1 0 fresh sage leaves, chopped
5 strips lemon zest
1 2 ounces fresh spinach, chopped
4 green onions, chopped

Place the beans, chicken broth, and beef broth in a large saucepan over medium heat. Add the onion, garlic, jalapeño, thyme, sage, and lemon zest. Bring to a boil. Lower heat and simmer slowly until the beans are almost tender, about 1 hour. Add the spinach and green onions; simmer 3 0 minutes more. Check for seasoning.

MAKES 8 TO 12 SERVINGS

VEGETABLE THYME GRATIN

Layering butternut squash, leeks, and tomatoes creates an array of yellow, white, and red.

2 pounds butternut squash
   or other winter squash
⅓ cup olive oil
1 teaspoon salt
¼ teaspoon finely ground pepper
3 medium leeks, white and
   light green parts, cleaned

2 pounds tomatoes, peeled,
   seeded, and chopped
1 teaspoon minced fresh thyme,
   or ½ teaspoon dried
1 cup (¼ pound) sharp
   cheddar cheese or grated Gruyère

Peel the squash and slice the flesh. Heat 3 tablespoons of the oil in a medium skillet. Add the squash and sauté over medium-high heat until lightly browned. Transfer to an oiled medium gratin dish or a baking dish. Sprinkle with ¼ teaspoon of the salt and a pinch of pepper.

Cut the leeks into thin slices. Heat 2 tablespoons of the oil in a skillet and add the leeks, ¼ teaspoon salt, and a pinch of pepper. Cook over low heat, stirring often, about 5 minutes, until softened. Spoon over squash in the gratin dish.

Heat the remaining 1 tablespoon oil in the pan that was used to cook the leeks. Add the tomatoes, thyme, remaining ½ teaspoon salt, and ¼ teaspoon pepper. Cook over medium-high heat, stirring often, about 15 minutes, until the tomato mixture is soft and thickened. Taste for seasoning.

Preheat the oven to 425 degrees. Spoon tomatoes over leeks. Sprinkle with cheese. Bake 15 minutes, until the cheese browns slightly. Serve immediately.

❋ NOTE: *This dish can be prepared up to 4 hours ahead and kept in the refrigerator. Bring to room temperature before baking.*

MAKES 6 TO 8 SERVINGS

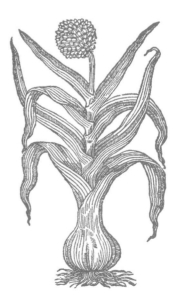

GARLIC

Medieval doctors carried garlic with them when making house calls.

In England garlic cloves were placed in the stockings of children

in the hope they would be protected from whooping cough.

CRISP HERBED POTATO CAKE

2¼ pounds russet potatoes
⅓ cup butter or margarine, melted
¾ teaspoon fresh or dried thyme leaves

¾ teaspoon fresh or dried
rosemary leaves, minced
Salt to taste

Preheat the oven to 450 degrees. Peel the potatoes and cut into ⅛-inch-thick slices. Combine the melted butter, rosemary, and thyme. Coat the inside of a 12-inch skillet or a 14-inch pizza pan with some of the herb butter. Neatly arrange the potato slices, overlapping, in concentric circles to form an even layer in the pan. Drizzle the remaining herb butter over the potatoes. Bake on the bottom rack in the oven until the potato cake is well browned and crisp on the top and bottom, about 1 hour. Lift with a spatula to see if it is done.

Invert a platter onto the skillet. Turn the potato cake onto the platter. Add salt to taste.

MAKES 4 SERVINGS

BARLEY WILD RICE MEDLEY ON A NEST OF SPINACH

⅓ cup pearl barley
¼ cup wild rice
2 cups chicken broth
1 tablespoon olive oil
8 ounces whole small button mushrooms,
    or quartered large mushrooms
⅓ cup chopped onion
1 clove garlic, minced

2 tablespoons sliced green onion
2 teaspoons fresh thyme
2 tablespoons minced fresh sweet marjoram
2 pounds tender spinach leaves,
    or 2 packages frozen spinach
2 tablespoons butter
Salt and pepper to taste
Fresh chives and marjoram leaves for garnish

Rinse the barley and rice. In a saucepan, combine the barley and rice with the broth. Bring to a boil. Reduce heat, cover, and simmer 45 minutes, until the liquid is absorbed.

In a large skillet, heat the oil and cook the mushrooms, onion, garlic, green onion, thyme, and marjoram for 7 minutes; set aside. In a large bowl, combine the barley and rice with the mushroom mixture.

To prepare the spinach nest, rinse the spinach in cold water. Place in a pot with just the water that clings to the leaves from rinsing. Cover and cook 3 to 10 minutes, until tender, stirring once or twice. Drain. Season with butter and salt and pepper to taste. (If fresh spinach is not available, just heat the frozen spinach.)

Arrange cooked spinach in a "nest," or hollow ring, on a platter. Place the mushroom-barley-rice mixture in the center. Garnish with minced fresh chives or garlic chives, a sprig or two of fresh marjoram, and several whole chive flowers. Or, sprinkle chive florets over the top.

SERVES 4 TO 6

ORANGE BASMATI WITH MINT

½ cup minced onion

4 tablespoons butter

1 ¼ cups basmati rice

4 tablespoons grated orange zest

Salt and pepper to taste

¾ cup orange juice

3 cups chicken broth

1 ½ tablespoons minced fresh mint leaves,
    or ½ teaspoon dried

½ cup slivered almonds, toasted

Preheat the oven to 350 degrees. In a casserole dish, sauté the onion in melted butter until soft; add the rice, orange zest, salt, pepper, orange juice, broth, and mint. Bake uncovered for 1 hour. Add more broth if necessary. Stir in the almonds for the last 10 minutes of baking.

MAKES 4 SERVINGS

CONFETTI RICE

So colorful, this rice looks like confetti: turmeric turns the rice bright yellow, the herbs add flecks of green, and the baby red and yellow tomatoes provide bursts of color.

2 cups chicken broth

1 tablespoon turmeric

¼ teaspoon cinnamon

1 cup basmati rice

¼ cup golden raisins

¼ cup dark raisins

2 tablespoons butter

2 tablespoons minced fresh parsley

2 tablespoons minced fresh chives
    or garlic chives

1 pint red and yellow baby pear
    or cherry tomatoes

Olive oil, enough to coat

Salt and pepper to taste

Combine the chicken broth, turmeric, and cinnamon in a small saucepan over medium heat. Add the rice; bring to a boil. Reduce heat, cover, and simmer until the liquid has evaporated, about 20 minutes. Add the raisins, butter, parsley, and chives.

If the tomatoes are large, halve them so they are bite-size. Toss the tomatoes with enough olive oil to coat, about 2 teaspoons. Season with salt and pepper. Spoon the tomatoes evenly over each serving of rice.

MAKES 4 SERVINGS

Plate 419.

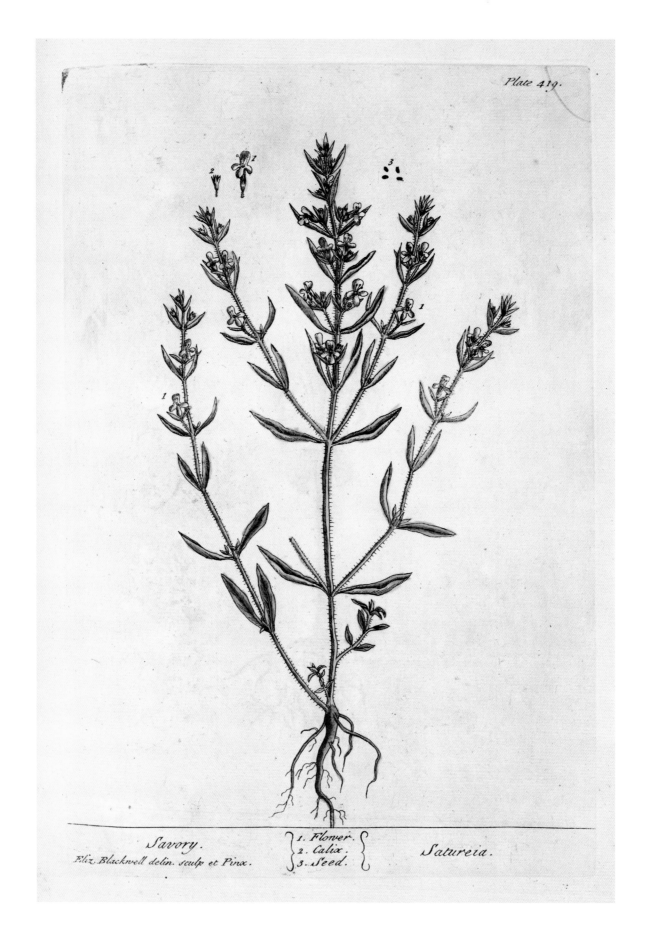

Savory.

Eliz. Blackwell delin. sculp et Pinx.

1. *Flower.*
2. *Calix.*
3. *Seed.*

Satureia.

ONION AND LEEK STRUDEL

This dish takes a bit of time to prepare—but it is worth it! Take advantage
of the make-ahead tips to prepare it, and enjoy the fancy, delicious result.

2½ tablespoons dried currants or raisins

2 tablespoons dry marsala

6 tablespoons (3 ounces) unsalted butter

1 tablespoon vegetable oil

2 cups thinly sliced onion

2 cups thinly sliced leeks
   (white and pale green parts only)

1 tablespoon light brown sugar

1 tablespoon lemon juice

1 tablespoon minced fresh summer savory,
   or 1 teaspoon dried

2 teaspoons minced fresh thyme

1 teaspoon grated lemon zest

⅛ teaspoon salt

Pepper to taste

3 slices white bread

5 sheets phyllo pastry

Soak the currants in marsala in a small bowl at least 2 hours, or overnight.

Melt 1 tablespoon of the butter with the oil in a heavy large skillet over medium-high heat. Add the onion and leeks. Sauté until just tender, about 5 minutes. Stir in the brown sugar, lemon juice, summer savory, thyme, and currant mixture. Reduce the heat to medium. Cover and cook until onions are very tender, stirring occasionally, about 10 minutes. Remove from heat. Stir in the lemon zest, salt, and pepper. Cool completely. (Filling can be prepared 1 day ahead; refrigerate. Bring the mixture to room temperature before continuing.)

Toast the bread until golden brown. Cool. Coarsely grind in a food processor.

Melt the remaining 5 tablespoons butter in a heavy small saucepan. Place a large sheet of waxed paper on the working surface. Place 1 phyllo sheet on top of the waxed paper. Cover the remainder with a damp towel and plastic wrap to prevent drying.

Brush the phyllo lightly with butter. Top with a second sheet of phyllo; brush with butter. Top with a third sheet of phyllo; brush with butter. Sprinkle 3 tablespoons bread crumbs over the buttered phyllo. Place a fourth sheet of phyllo on the bread crumbs. Brush with butter and sprinkle 3 tablespoons bread crumbs. Top with the fifth phyllo sheet. Brush the phyllo with butter and sprinkle 3 tablespoons bread crumbs.

Spoon the onion filling along one long side of the 5 layers of pastry in a 3-inch-wide strip, beginning 1½ inches in from one long side and leaving a 1-inch border on the short sides. Fold the short sides in over the filling. Brush the folded borders with butter. Starting at the filled side, gently roll the pastry up jelly roll–style, forming a strudel.

Brush the top, ends, and sides of the strudel with butter. Transfer to a buttered baking sheet, seam side down. Using a serrated knife, make diagonal slits in the pastry (do not cut through to the filling) 2 inches apart, forming 6 sections. (This can be prepared 2 hours ahead. Cover loosely with plastic and refrigerate.)

Position a rack in the center of the oven and preheat to 375 degrees. Bake the strudel until golden brown and crisp, about 30 minutes. Cool 30 minutes on a rack. Cut strudel at the slits and serve.

MAKES 6 SERVINGS

Plate 159.

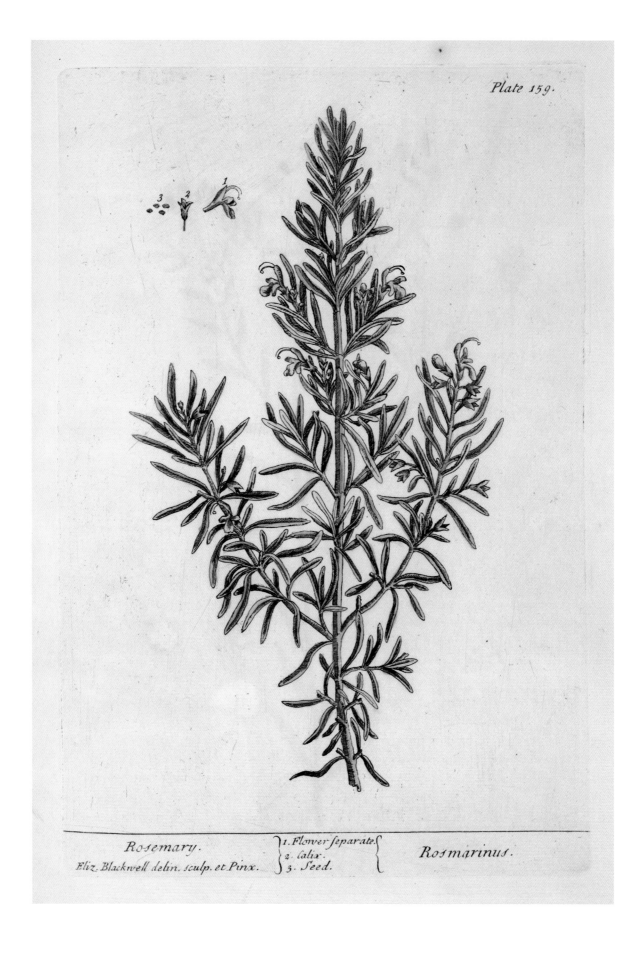

Rosemary.

Eliz. Blackwell delin. sculp. et Pinx.

1. *Flower separate.*
2. *Calix.*
3. *Seed.*

Rosmarinus.

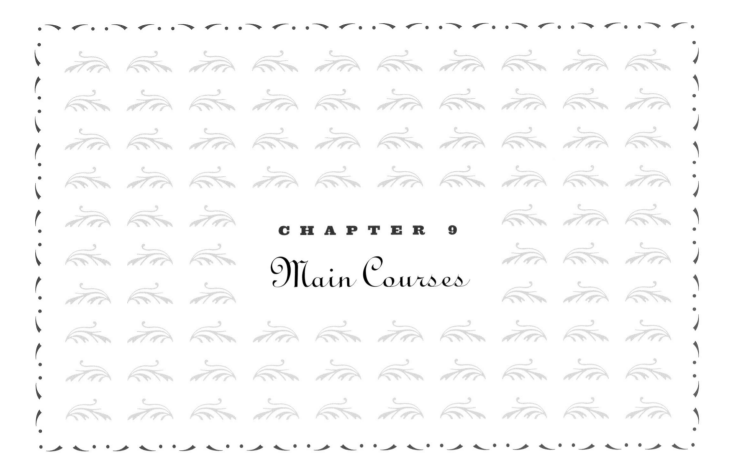

CHAPTER 9

Main Courses

Generally speaking, when it comes to dinner, the star of the show is the main course. Usually it's the protein-bearing dish—if not meat or fish, then cheese, eggs, beans, or another vegetable protein source. Frequently, the main course sets a theme, and it often requires the most preparation time and expense. No wonder that when we plan a meal, we decide upon the main dish first, then plan the other components around it!

No strictly vegetarian entrées appear in this chapter, but this is not to imply that only meat, chicken, or fish is appropriate for a main course. On the contrary, herbs have a special affinity for other items in the vegetable kingdom. Many excellent vegetarian entrées can be found in the pasta, salads, and vegetables chapters, so if you're a vegetarian, ignore this chapter and move on to the others.

Fish

BAKED SALMON WITH WILD RICE AND CHARDONNAY TARRAGON SAUCE

Serve with sautéed baby carrots with mint leaves.

4 ounces wild rice
2 cups chicken broth
2 salmon fillets, about 4 pounds
3 shallots, minced
3 tablespoons unsalted butter
¾ pound mushrooms, finely chopped

2 cups spinach leaves, chopped
2 teaspoons minced fresh tarragon,
   or more to taste
½ teaspoon ground nutmeg
Salt and pepper to taste
Fresh tarragon sprigs for garnish
Chardonnay Tarragon Sauce (see below)

❧ HERB RUBS ❧

An herb rub is easy to make and adds flavor to roasted or grilled meats or fish. Combine an assortment of dried herbs, such as any of the various thymes, sweet marjoram, oregano, tarragon, rosemary, and perhaps some fennel seed, freshly ground pepper, dried English lavender buds, or grated lemon rind in a small bowl. To form a savory crust, make a thick paste by adding some olive oil. Up to one hour before cooking, rub the mixture all over the meat or fish.

Cook the wild rice according to package directions, using chicken broth rather than water. Set aside. Cut a piece of parchment paper or aluminum foil the length and width of a baking dish, large enough to hold both salmon fillets. Butter one side of the paper and set in the dish buttered side up. Place the salmon fillets on top of the paper and set aside.

Preheat the oven to 350 degrees. In a large skillet, sauté the shallots in melted butter until translucent, about 2 to 3 minutes. Add the mushrooms and cook until the mixture thickens and the mushroom liquid has cooked away, about 10 to 15 minutes. Add the chopped spinach and cook until tender, about 3 minutes. Blend in the cooked wild rice, tarragon, and nutmeg. Season to taste with salt and pepper.

Spread the spinach-rice mixture over both fillets. Cover each with aluminum foil; bake until a knife inserted into the thickest part of fillet reveals that the flesh is flaky, about 20 minutes.

To serve, arrange fillets on a serving platter; cut each fillet in half lengthwise and then crosswise into 1½-inch strips. Garnish with tarragon sprigs and serve with Chardonnay Tarragon Sauce.

MAKES 12 SERVINGS

Chardonnay Tarragon Sauce

4 medium shallots, minced	2 to 3 tablespoons Creole
1 cup chardonnay	or whole seed mustard
2 cups chicken broth	2 tablespoons minced fresh tarragon
1½ cups cream	Salt and pepper to taste

In a medium saucepan, combine the shallots, wine, and broth. Simmer over medium-high heat until reduced to 1 cup, about 25 to 35 minutes. Strain through a sieve, pressing shallots to extract juices. Return to the saucepan and whisk in cream and mustard. Cook, stirring occasionally, over medium heat until thickened, 10 to 20 minutes. Remove from heat, whisk in the tarragon, and season with salt and pepper.

MAKES 1 1/2 CUPS

SALMON IN BASIL CREAM

One taste of this delicious sauce will make you think that you're in France. Serve with steamed rice or fresh noodles.

1 pound salmon fillet	¾ cup dry vermouth
1½ tablespoons butter	⅓ cup light cream
3 shallots	1 tablespoon lemon juice
1 garlic clove, minced	¼ teaspoon pepper
1½ cups minced fresh basil	Salt to taste
¼ cup minced fresh parsley	

Cut the salmon into 4 equal pieces. Melt the butter in a large skillet; sear the salmon 2 to 3 minutes on each side. If the salmon is thick, you can break it into pieces or increase the cooking time to reach the desired doneness. Remove from the pan and keep warm. Reduce heat to low; add the shallots and garlic and cook, stirring, 5 minutes. Add the basil, parsley, vermouth, cream, lemon juice, pepper, and salt to the pan and cook over medium heat until reduced by half, stirring frequently. Add more salt and pepper as needed. Reheat the fish slightly in the sauce and serve.

MAKES 4 SERVINGS

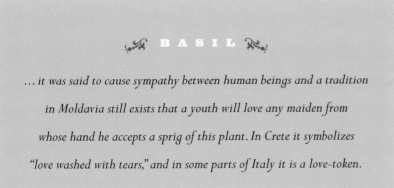

BASIL

… it was said to cause sympathy between human beings and a tradition in Moldavia still exists that a youth will love any maiden from whose hand he accepts a sprig of this plant. In Crete it symbolizes "love washed with tears," and in some parts of Italy it is a love-token.

GRIEVE

FISH FILLETS IN TARRAGON SAUCE

2 cloves garlic, minced
1 green onion, thinly sliced
3 tablespoons olive oil
2 cups fresh tomatoes, peeled, seeded, and chopped

1 teaspoon minced fresh tarragon leaves, plus ½ teaspoon per fillet for garnish
1 tablespoon balsamic vinegar
⅛ teaspoon freshly ground black pepper
1 pound sole fillets

Combine the garlic, green onion, and oil in a 3-quart microwave-safe casserole. Cover with waxed paper and microwave on high 1 minute.

Stir in the tomatoes, tarragon, vinegar, and pepper; cover and microwave on high for 3 to 4 minutes, until heated through.

If the fish fillets are wider than 2 to 3 inches, cut in half lengthwise. Fold the thinner ends of each fillet under the thicker part in the center. Place the folded fish in the sauce around the outer rim of the casserole. Cover again and microwave on high until the fish is done, 3 to 5 minutes. To serve, sprinkle ½ teaspoon minced fresh tarragon over each fillet. Serve over steamed rice.

NOTE: *Catfish or flounder can also be used.*

MAKES 4 SERVINGS

Chicken

MOROCCAN CHICKEN PIE

This version of the bastilla, *a Moroccan savory pie composed of chicken and spices encased in phyllo, takes a while to assemble. You can make it up to 2 days ahead if you store it in the refrigerator before baking.*

Filling

2 tablespoons olive oil
2 pounds dark chicken meat, boned and skinned
1½ cups chopped onion
3 cloves garlic, finely chopped
1 teaspoon minced fresh ginger
3 teaspoons ground cinnamon
1½ teaspoons ground cumin
1 teaspoon ground coriander

½ teaspoon cayenne
¾ teaspoon turmeric
¼ teaspoon crushed saffron threads
2 cups reduced sodium chicken broth
2½ tablespoons minced fresh cilantro
1½ tablespoons minced fresh parsley
7 large eggs, lightly beaten
1 teaspoon salt
½ teaspoon freshly ground black pepper

Topping

  1½ cups slivered blanched almonds
  2 tablespoons sugar
  2 teaspoons ground cinnamon

24 frozen phyllo sheets,
   thawed (17 × 12 inches)
1 cup (½ pound) butter, melted
Powdered sugar (optional)
Ground cinnamon (optional)

In a large skillet or 5-quart Dutch oven, heat 1 tablespoon of the olive oil over medium-high heat. Sauté the chicken until golden brown on all sides, about 5 minutes. Remove the chicken and set aside.

In the same skillet, add the onion, garlic, ginger, and remaining 1 tablespoon oil; sauté, stirring constantly, just until the onions are translucent. Stir in the cinnamon, cumin, coriander, cayenne, turmeric, and saffron. Reduce the heat to low and cook, stirring constantly, until the onions are completely coated with the spices, about 3 minutes.

Increase the heat to high. Add the broth, cilantro, and parsley to the skillet with the onion mixture. Heat to boiling, stirring to combine. Return the chicken to the skillet, cover, reduce heat to low, and simmer 30 minutes, until the chicken is tender.

Transfer the chicken from the skillet to a plate; set aside to cool. Continue to cook the onion mixture, covered, until almost dry, about 15 minutes. Add the eggs, salt, and pepper to the onion mixture. Cook until soft curds form, about 3 minutes. Remove the skillet from the heat and set aside the onion-egg mixture to cool.

To prepare the topping, heat the oven to 375 degrees. Spread the almonds on an ungreased baking sheet and place in the oven for 7 minutes, until lightly toasted. In a food processor with the chopping blade, process the almonds with the sugar and cinnamon.

When the chicken is cool enough to handle, tear it into 2-inch-long strips.

To assemble the pie, place the phyllo between 2 sheets of waxed paper, then cover with a damp towel. Brush a 12-inch pizza pan with melted butter. Remove 1 sheet of phyllo and place on the pan, letting the edges hang over the rim. Brush the phyllo sheet with butter, keeping the other sheets covered with the damp towel. Working quickly, stack and butter 11 more sheets, arranging them in the pan in an overlapping, circular fashion, like a pinwheel.

In the center of the phyllo, in even layers, arrange half of the topping, half of the onion-egg mixture, all of the chicken strips, the remaining onion-egg mixture, and the remaining topping. Fold overhanging phyllo over the top of the pie and brush with butter.

Continue to butter and arrange the remaining 12 phyllo sheets in the same pinwheel fashion over the top of the pie. Carefully tuck the overhanging ends underneath it. Brush the top and sides of the pie with butter. Cover loosely with foil. At this point, the pie can be refrigerated for up to 2 days.

Preheat the oven to 350 degrees. Bake the pie 20 minutes, until golden. If the pie has been chilled, bake 5 to 10 minutes longer. Place a baking sheet or another 12-inch pizza pan over the pie and invert. Return to the oven on the new pan and bake 25 minutes longer, until crisp and golden.

If desired, sprinkle confectioners' sugar and ground cinnamon in stripes on top of the pie.

MAKES 12 SERVINGS

Plate 176.

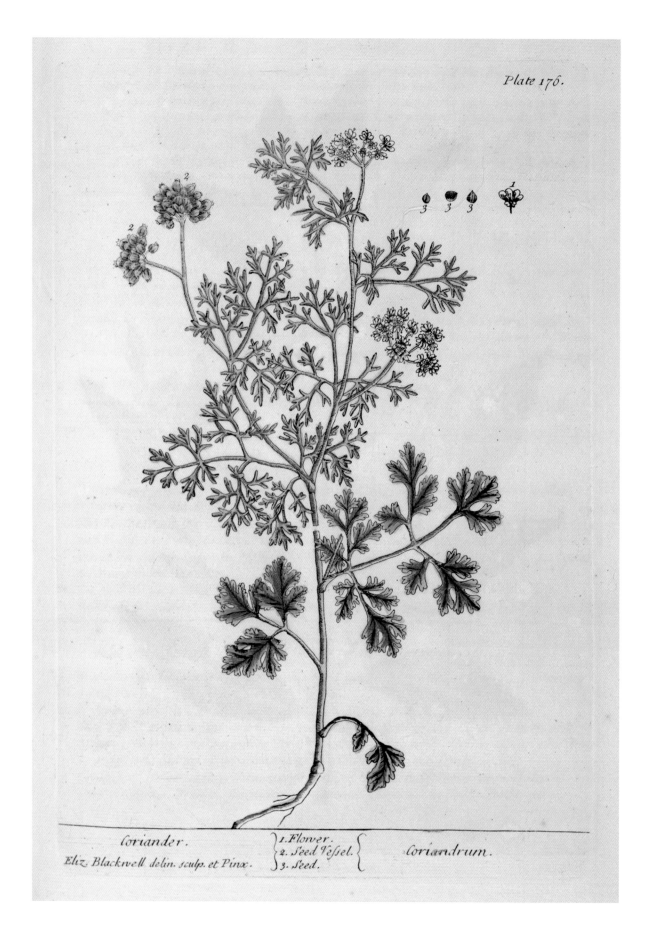

Coriander.

Eliz. Blackwell delin. sculp. et Pinx.

1. Flower.
2. Seed Vessel.
3. Seed.

Coriandrum.

BAKED TARRAGON CHICKEN IN YOGURT SAUCE

Delicious and easy to make. Tarragon also combines well with citrus flavor. Fresh broccoli or asparagus would make a good accompaniment, or serve a rice pilaf to soak up some of the sauce.

¼ cup butter or margarine
8 boneless, skinless chicken breasts, halved
½ cup slivered almonds
2 tablespoons flour
½ cup chicken broth
½ cup yogurt
2 tablespoons white wine
1 teaspoon grated orange or lemon zest
2 teaspoons minced fresh tarragon,
   or 1 teaspoon dried
½ teaspoon salt
⅛ teaspoon pepper
½ cup sliced raw mushrooms

TARRAGON

Tarragon is hot and drie in the third degree, and not to be eaten alone in sallades, but ioyned with other herbes, as Lettuce, Purslain, and such like, that it may also temper the coldness of them, like as Rocket doth, neither doe we know what other use this herbe hath.

GERARD

Preheat the oven to 350 degrees. Melt 1 tablespoon of the butter in a large shallow baking pan; arrange the chicken breasts in the pan. Bake for 30 minutes.

Melt the rest of the butter in a saucepan. Stir in the almonds and heat over medium heat until golden brown. Remove the almonds and set aside. Stir flour into the melted butter and cook gently 1 to 2 minutes. Stir in the broth and cook until the mixture thickens. Blend in the yogurt, wine, zest, tarragon, salt, and pepper.

Turn the chicken breasts over. Cover with sliced mushrooms and almonds; pour sauce over the tops. Bake uncovered for 20 minutes, until tender. Place under the broiler for about 2 minutes to brown the tops. Serve with rice.

MAKES 8 SERVINGS

CORIANDER

Coriander was listed among the medicinal plants mentioned in the Papyrus of Thebes, written in 1552 B.C.

PHYLLO-WRAPPED HERBED CHICKEN BREASTS

Serve the chicken packets on a bed of chive leaves or tarragon sprigs.

1 ½ cups mayonnaise
1 cup chopped green onion
⅓ cup lemon juice
¼ cup sour cream
2 cloves garlic, minced
2 teaspoons dried or 1 tablespoon
   minced fresh tarragon
1 tablespoon minced fresh garlic chives

12 boneless, skinless chicken breasts
Salt and pepper to taste
24 frozen phyllo sheets, thawed
⅔ cup butter, melted
⅓ cup grated Parmesan cheese
Chive blossoms and sprigs
   of fresh tarragon for garnish

Preheat oven to 375 degrees. Combine the mayonnaise, green onion, lemon juice, sour cream, garlic, tarragon, and garlic chives. Lightly sprinkle the chicken breasts with salt and pepper.

For each chicken breast, place 2 sheets of phyllo dough together on a damp towel; brush the top with melted butter. Spread 1 ½ tablespoons sauce on each side of the chicken breast. Place the chicken in one corner of the phyllo and fold the corner over; fold the sides in, and roll to form a packet enclosing the chicken.

Place on an ungreased baking sheet. Brush the tops of the packets lightly with butter and sprinkle with Parmesan cheese. Bake for 20 to 25 minutes until golden. To serve, garnish with chive blossoms and sprigs of fresh tarragon.

MAKES 12 SERVINGS

GRILLED CHICKEN KABOBS WITH ANISE AND MINT

The woody stems of rosemary with leaves removed, having been soaked
for at least an hour in water, make wonderful skewers for any kind of kabobs.

1 whole boneless, skinless chicken breast,
   about 1 ½ pounds
1 teaspoon ground anise seeds
1 tablespoon minced fresh mint,
   or 2 teaspoons dried
½ cup lemon juice
½ cup grated or puréed onion

Freshly ground black pepper
   and kosher salt to taste
8 rosemary stems or bamboo skewers
1 large red bell pepper, stemmed,
   seeded, and cut into 1 ½-inch pieces
1 portobello mushroom, cut into ¼-inch
   slices, or 6 small white button mushrooms
1 large onion, cut into 1 ½-inch pieces
Olive oil spray

Trim any visible fat from the chicken. Cut the meat into 1½-inch pieces and place in a bowl. Add the anise seeds, mint, lemon juice, grated onion, and pepper and salt to taste. Toss to coat the meat. Cover and set aside for 30 minutes, or refrigerate overnight.

Preheat a charcoal grill or an oven broiler. Soak rosemary stems or bamboo skewers in water.

Add the bell pepper, mushroom, and onion to the chicken. Toss to coat the vegetables with the marinade. Alternating the vegetables with the chicken, thread pieces on the skewers. Reserve the marinade. Spray with olive oil.

If barbecuing, arrange the skewers on the rack. If broiling, put the skewers on the broiler pan and place under the broiler, 4 to 5 inches from the heat. Cook for 8 minutes, turning and basting with the marinade. Do not overcook, because chicken dries out easily. Serve 2 skewers per person on individual plates. Serve immediately.

MAKES 4 SERVINGS

ROASTED CHICKEN WITH HERBES DE PROVENCE

Double or triple the ingredients to make 4 to 6 servings of this easy recipe.

2 whole chicken legs (with thighs), skinned and trimmed of any visible fat
2 teaspoons olive oil
2 teaspoons minced garlic
1 teaspoon dried herbes de Provence (see page 5)

¼ teaspoon ground cinnamon
½ teaspoon ground black pepper
¼ teaspoon salt
Water-oil mist
2 sprigs of herbs (sage, rosemary, or thyme) for garnish

Preheat oven to 375 degrees. Place the chicken legs in a shallow dish. Combine the olive oil, garlic, herbes de Provence, cinnamon, pepper, and salt. Rub mixture over the chicken and set aside for 15 minutes.

Place the legs on a roasting pan and place in the middle of the oven. Roast until the chicken is tender, 45 to 60 minutes. Spray with water-oil mist every 15 to 20 minutes, at least twice during roasting. Serve warm, or at room temperature. Garnish with sprigs of herbs.

❧ NOTE: *To make the water-oil mist, put equal amounts of olive oil and water in a spray bottle. Shake well before using.*

MAKES 2 SERVINGS

Meat

ROAST PORK TENDERLOIN WITH ORANGE ROSEMARY BUTTER

Excellent with mashed potatoes or steamed rice.

Orange Rosemary Butter
½ cup (4 ounces) butter, at room temperature
3 tablespoons frozen orange juice
   concentrate, thawed
1 tablespoon minced orange zest
1 ½ tablespoons finely chopped fresh
   rosemary, or 2 teaspoons dried
⅛ teaspoon salt
⅛ teaspoon white pepper

Tenderloins
4 (8-ounce) pork tenderloins,
   trimmed of excess fat
3 teaspoons slivered garlic cloves
3 teaspoons slivered orange zest
Salt and freshly ground black pepper to taste
1 cup chicken broth
Fresh rosemary sprigs for garnish (optional)

> ### ❧ ROSEMARY ❧
>
> *It helps a weak memory, and quickens*
> *the senses. . . . It helps dim eyes, and*
> *procures a clear sight, the flowers thereof*
> *if taken all the while it is flowering, every*
> *morning fasting, with bread and salt.*
>
> CULPEPER

To make the orange rosemary butter, combine the butter, orange juice concentrate, zest, rosemary, salt, and pepper until well blended. Store covered in the refrigerator. Prepare at least 1 day ahead to allow the flavors to blend.

When ready to cook the tenderloins, make slits over the surface of each one with a sharp paring knife. Insert the garlic and orange zest slivers into the slits.

Preheat the oven to 350 degrees. Melt 2 tablespoons of the orange rosemary butter in a large skillet over medium heat. When hot, brown the tenderloins evenly, turning often, 5 to 7 minutes. Place the tenderloins on a rack in a roasting pan and pour any drippings from the skillet into the roasting pan. Season the tenderloins with salt and pepper to taste. Spread 1 teaspoon orange rosemary butter over each. Pour chicken broth into the pan. Roast, uncovered, until a meat thermometer registers between 155 and 160 degrees, 20 to 25 minutes.

Transfer the pork to a serving platter. Cover loosely with aluminum foil. Pour the liquid from the roasting pan into a small heavy saucepan. Cook over medium-high heat until the mixture is reduced by half. Whisk in the remaining orange rosemary butter and simmer, stirring constantly, on low heat for 5 minutes. Taste the sauce, and season with salt and pepper if needed.

Slice the pork in ½-inch-thick slices and serve. Drizzle with sauce and garnish with fresh rosemary sprigs.

MAKES 8 TO 10 SERVINGS

PLUM-GRILLED PORK CHOPS

Pork and plums pair well in this summer fare.

1 tablespoon minced fresh sage
1 tablespoon minced fresh thyme
½ teaspoon salt
½ teaspoon sugar
¼ teaspoon paprika
6 pork chops, ½ inch thick
6 medium red plums, pitted and halved
¼ cup honey
2 tablespoons fresh lime juice
1 teaspoon Dijon mustard
4 shallots, finely diced and puréed
12 sprigs of sage or thyme for garnish

Combine the sage, thyme, salt, sugar, and paprika in a small bowl. Place the pork chops in a shallow baking dish and sprinkle both sides with the dry herb mixture. Cover and refrigerate 1 to 2 hours.

Heat charcoal in an outdoor grill over medium heat. Lightly oil the grill rack and place it 4 inches above the coals. Grill the chops 4 minutes on each side, until done.

Place the plums on the grill and cook, turning often, until soft and slightly browned. Combine the honey, lime juice, mustard, and shallots. Brush the chops and plums with part of the honey mixture to glaze. Transfer to a serving platter. Drizzle with the remaining honey sauce. Garnish with sage or thyme sprigs.

MAKES 6 SERVINGS

SAGE

Bruse Sage and put it into a little bag, and put it into a quart of wine at night, and then strein it and use it as Sage wine to consume flegme, and to comfort the brain and sinews. LANGHAM

HERB-ENCRUSTED PORK TENDERLOIN WITH RASPBERRY SAUCE

Handle the coated tenderloins gently to keep the herb crusts intact.

Tenderloins

3 (1-pound) or 6 (8-ounce) pork tenderloins

2 cloves garlic, crushed

1 tablespoon salt

1 tablespoon cracked pepper

1 cup Dijon mustard

¼ cup brandy

¼ cup maple syrup

2 tablespoons raspberry vinegar
(add 1 teaspoon English lavender
flowers, if available)

1 tablespoon minced fresh rosemary

1 tablespoon minced fresh parsley

1 tablespoon minced fresh sage

1 tablespoon minced fresh thyme

1 tablespoon minced fresh marjoram

2 cups cracker crumbs or dried bread crumbs

2 tablespoons olive oil

Sauce

1 cup merlot

¼ cup raspberry liqueur
(Chambord or equivalent)

¼ cup beef or veal broth

1 cup cream

¼ cup maple syrup

1 tablespoon Dijon mustard

Trim the tenderloins and rub with the garlic, salt, and cracked pepper. Combine the mustard, brandy, maple syrup, raspberry vinegar, rosemary, parsley, sage, thyme, and marjoram. Spread the mustard-herb mixture over the tenderloins and roll them in the cracker crumbs. Marinate in the refrigerator for at least 30 minutes, or overnight.

Preheat the oven to 400 degrees. Heat a skillet and add the oil. Brown the tenderloins for 2 minutes on each side. Watch carefully to avoid burning the crumbs. Place the tenderloins in a baking dish and roast. The 8-ounce loins will need 12 to 18 minutes, and the 1-pound tenderloins will need 30 to 45 minutes. The small end tips will roast faster and should be cut off after 12 to 15 minutes.

While the loins are roasting, combine the merlot, raspberry liqueur, and broth in a saucepan. Bring to a boil and reduce the mixture by two thirds (about 1 cup), until it is syrupy and forms large bubbles. Take care not to let it burn. Reduce heat, and add the cream, syrup, and mustard. Increase heat to medium, and cook the sauce until reduced by half, about 20 minutes.

To serve, slice the tenderloins and top with the raspberry sauce.

MAKES 8 SERVINGS

PORK CUTLETS ON A BED OF CABBAGE

The small amount of fennel seeds adds a haunting flavor to the sauce.

1 tablespoon vegetable oil
8 ounces pork cutlets, chops,
    or tenderloin, cut ¾ inch thick
¼ cup chopped onion
⅛ teaspoon fennel seeds, crushed
1/16 teaspoon white pepper
1 cup chicken broth
2 cups thinly shredded cabbage
½ cup half-and-half
1 tablespoon all-purpose flour
Ground nutmeg to taste

Heat a large skillet over medium heat. Add the oil and pork and cook, covered, until browned, about 2 minutes on each side. Remove the pork. Add the onion and brown for 2 minutes. Stir in the fennel seeds and white pepper and sauté for 1 minute. Stir in the chicken broth and bring to a simmer. Add the pork and cook, covered, until it is tender, about 45 minutes.

Transfer the pork to a serving platter, leaving the onion mixture in the skillet. Add the cabbage to the onions, stir well, and cook, covered, 5 minutes. Mix the half-and-half and flour together, then stir into the cabbage mixture; cook, covered, until the cabbage is tender, about 4 minutes. Place the cabbage-onion mixture on a serving platter. Top with pork cutlets. Sprinkle lightly with nutmeg.

MAKES 2 SERVINGS

✣ FENNEL ✣

Heart burning, chew crops of Fennill, and such downe the juyce and spit out the rest. Belly windy, seethe powder of the seedes of Fennill, Annise, and Cummin in wine, and drinke it.

LANGHAM

PINTO BEAN, SAUSAGE, AND FENNEL GRATIN

1 pound dried pinto or red kidney beans,
  soaked overnight
1 pound Italian sausage, casings removed
  and discarded
1 tablespoon olive oil
2 cups finely chopped onion
3 cups thinly sliced fennel bulb (1 large bulb)
1 large red bell pepper, cut into thin strips
1 tablespoon minced fresh basil
1 tablespoon minced fresh thyme

Salt and pepper to taste
1 cup chicken broth
2 (14-ounce) cans artichoke hearts
  or bottoms, rinsed and drained
½ cup minced fresh parsley
½ cup red wine
1 cup fresh bread crumbs
½ cup Parmesan cheese
¼ cup (2 ounces) unsalted butter,
  cut into bits

In a large pot, combine the beans with enough cold water to cover them by 2 inches; simmer covered for 1 to 1½ hours, until tender. Drain the beans in a colander set over a large bowl; reserve the cooking liquid.

Butter a 4-quart 15 × 10 × 2-inch gratin dish. In a large heavy skillet, cook the sausage over moderate heat, stirring and breaking up any large lumps, until cooked through. Transfer with a slotted spoon to a large bowl. Add the oil to the skillet.

Cook the onion, fennel, bell pepper, basil, thyme, salt, and pepper over medium heat, stirring, until the vegetables have softened. Add the broth and simmer, covered, for 5 to 10 minutes, until the vegetables are tender.

Cut the artichoke hearts into 8 pieces each. In a blender, purée 1½ cups of the cooked beans with 1 cup of the reserved cooking liquid. Add the purée, remaining cooked beans, sausage, artichoke hearts, parsley, and wine to the vegetable mixture; transfer to the gratin dish.

Preheat the oven to 350 degrees. In a small bowl, combine the bread crumbs and Parmesan cheese; sprinkle the mixture evenly over the gratin. Dot the gratin with the cut-up butter. Bake in the middle of the oven for 45 to 50 minutes, until the top is golden.

MAKES 10 SERVINGS

WILD THYME

I know a bank where the wild thyme blows,

Where oxlips and the nodding violet grows;

Quite over-canopied with lush woodbine,

With sweet musk-roses and with eglantine . . .

SHAKESPEARE
A Midsummer Night's Dream

Shakespeare refers to the "bank where the wild thyme blows" in designating where Titania, the Queen of the Fairies, could be found napping. Thyme was believed to be a plant much loved by fairies and one in which they would dwell. Wild thyme was a creeping form which is in all respects diminutive in scale, quite appropriate for the "little folk."

RACK OF LAMB RUBBED WITH PARSLEY, SAGE, ROSEMARY, AND THYME

The inspiration for this recipe is doubtless "Scarborough Faire," the traditional English song made famous by the 1960s musical duo Simon and Garfunkel.

4 cloves garlic, crushed and minced
8 parsley sprigs, finely chopped
¼ cup olive oil
2 teaspoons salt
2 teaspoons coarsely ground pepper
2 teaspoons dried sage

2 teaspoons dried rosemary
2 teaspoons dried thyme
¼ cup flour
1½ cups dry white wine
1 rack of lamb (2 to 4 pounds)

Combine the garlic, parsley, oil, salt, and pepper in a small bowl and set aside. Combine the sage, rosemary, thyme, and flour in a separate small bowl and set aside. Place the wine in a shallow open roasting pan. Place a rack in the roasting pan and set aside.

Place the lamb on a baking sheet. Stir the oil-garlic mixture; pour it over the lamb, rubbing over the entire piece. Transfer the rack to a sheet of waxed paper. Wash and dry hands thoroughly before proceeding to the next step.

Sprinkle the herb-flour mixture over the chop side of the rack of lamb, patting it into the oil mixture as you sprinkle. Use all of the dry mixture, including any that accumulates on the waxed paper.

Place the lamb on the roasting rack. Insert a meat thermometer into the thickest part of the meat. Roast at 325 degrees for 1½ to 2½ hours, until the meat thermometer registers 175 to 180 degrees. Transfer to a serving platter to rest 10 minutes. Carve and serve.

MAKES 4 TO 6 SERVINGS

❀ NOTE: *For a 4- to 6-pound leg of lamb, double the oil and seasoning mixtures. Coat the entire leg of lamb with both mixtures, following the same procedure. Roast at 325 degrees for 2½ to 3½ hours, until the meat thermometer registers 175 to 180 degrees. Makes 6 to 10 servings, depending on weight.*

LAMB PIE WITH HERB CRUST

A great comfort food for Sunday night supper! The crust and the filling can be made
a day ahead and refrigerated until you are ready to assemble and bake the pie.

Crust

1¼ cups all-purpose flour

¼ teaspoon salt

2 teaspoons chopped fresh chives

1 tablespoon minced fresh parsley

1 teaspoon chopped fresh dill,
   or ½ teaspoon dried

1 (3-ounce) package cream cheese

½ cup butter or margarine

1 tablespoon ice water

1 egg yolk beaten with 1 teaspoon milk

Filling

1 large garlic clove, chopped

3 tablespoons olive oil

3 pounds boneless lamb shoulder,
   trimmed and cut into 1½-inch cubes

Salt and pepper to taste

3 tablespoons flour

2 cups dry white wine, red wine,
   or bouillon, alone or combined

1 (3- to 4-inch) sprig fresh rosemary,
   or 2 teaspoons dried

1 bay leaf

12 to 18 small white onions, parboiled if fresh

1 to 2 cups peas, fresh or frozen

In a food processor or by hand, mix the flour, salt, chives, parsley, and dill. Cut in the cream cheese and butter; mix until the dough holds together in a ball, adding the ice water a little at a time. Form into a flattened ball and wrap in wax paper or plastic wrap. Chill for up to 24 hours.

Sauté the garlic in olive oil over medium heat until golden. Remove garlic and set aside. Sprinkle the lamb with salt and pepper; brown over medium-high heat. Lower the heat to medium and stir in the flour, coating the meat. Add the wine and/or bouillon and stir up any browned bits sticking to the pan. Add the rosemary, bay leaf, white onions, and peas and simmer over low heat until meat is tender, about 20 minutes. Remove bay leaf and stems of rosemary. When the mixture is cool, store in a covered container in the refrigerator until ready to assemble or continue on.

Remove the herb crust and lamb mixture from the refrigerator about 2 hours before ready to bake. Preheat the oven to 400 degrees. Place lamb mixture in a 1½- to 2-quart buttered baking dish. On a lightly floured board, roll the pie crust to a thickness of about ¼ inch. Cut into 1-inch strips. Arrange lattice fashion on the pie, trimming the ends. Glaze the top with an egg yolk beaten with a teaspoon of milk. Bake in the preheated oven 15 to 20 minutes or until the crust is golden brown.

SERVES 4 TO 6

HERBED TRI-TIP
WITH ROSEMARY BUTTER

*A popular entrée at the Huntington restaurant. The robust flavor of rosemary pairs well with beef.
Use the same butter and marinade with a barbecued, butterflied leg of lamb.*

Rosemary Butter
½ pound butter
1 tablespoon chopped shallots
¼ cup beef stock
2 tablespoons fresh rosemary, chopped

Marinade
1 tablespoon fresh rosemary, chopped
2 (3-inch) sprigs fresh thyme
¼ cup olive oil
⅓ cup chopped onion

2 pounds tri-tip, trimmed of fat
Salt and pepper to taste

For the rosemary butter, melt 1 tablespoon of the butter in a heavy medium saucepan over medium heat. Add the shallots and cook until tender, about 3 minutes. Stir in the beef stock and rosemary. Bring to a boil for 10 minutes. Lower the heat and add the rest of the butter. Season to taste.

For the marinade, combine the rosemary, thyme, olive oil, and onion in a zippered plastic bag. Add the meat and marinate for at least 1 hour. Prepare the barbecue or broiler, using high heat. Remove the meat from the marinade and pat dry. Sprinkle the meat with salt and pepper. Grill or boil the meat to desired doneness. Let rest 5 to 8 minutes before slicing. Slice and dress with the rosemary butter.

SERVES 6 TO 8

ROSEMARY

*Seethe much rosemary and bathe therein, to make
thee lusty, lively, joyfull, likeing, and yongly.*

LANGHAM

Plate 354.

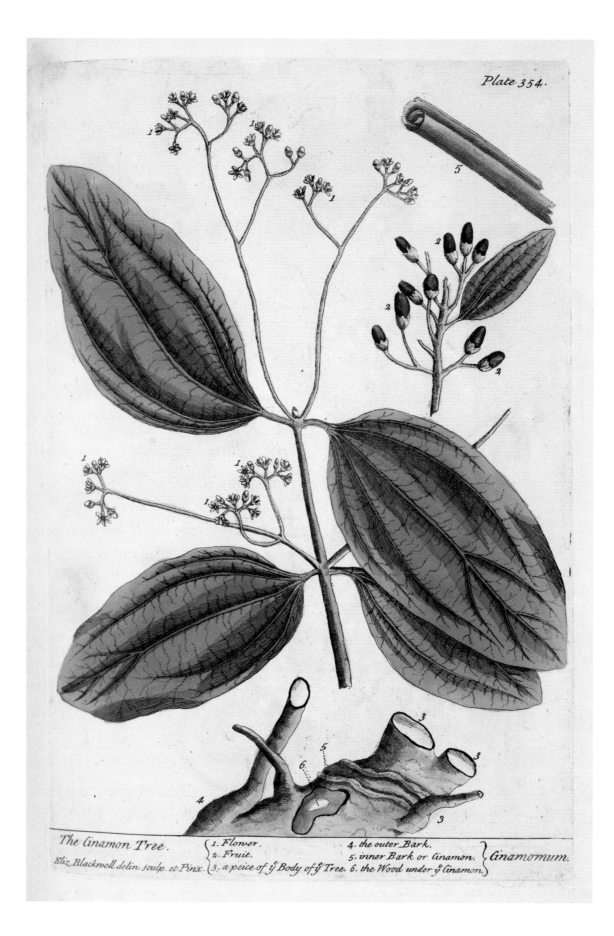

The Cinamon Tree.

Eliz. Blackwell delin. sculp. et Pinx.

1. Flower.
2. Fruit.
3. a peice of ÿ Body of ÿ Tree.
4. the outer Bark.
5. inner Bark or Cinamon.
6. the Wood under ÿ Cinamon.

Cinamomum.

CHAPTER 10

Desserts

Most herbs are savory, but several are "sweet," and the following are great for desserts:

CINNAMON BASIL ❧ GINGER ❧ LEMON BALM ❧ LEMON BASIL
LEMON THYME ❧ LEMON VERBENA ❧ LICORICE BASIL
MARJORAM ❧ MINT ❧ ROSELLE ❧ ROSE PETALS
SAFFRON ❧ SWEET WOODRUFF ❧ TARRAGON

"Seed herbs" are also traditionally found in desserts and confections: anise, caraway, coriander, fennel, nigella, and poppy.

Or, make sweet flowers into an infusion to flavor desserts. Other cultures use roses, lavender, and orange blossoms, and flowers are just beginning to be appreciated in the United States. Most recently, imaginative culinary artists have even been using rosemary in desserts with wonderful results.

ROSE WATER

4 cups fresh, fragrant, unsprayed rose petals   Enough water to cover petals

Wash and drain the rose petals in cold running water. Place the petals in a glass jar and add enough boiling water to cover. Cool for 5 minutes, then cover and set aside for 48 hours, shaking the jar occasionally. Strain.

ROSE SYRUP

Rose water (see previous recipe)   2 cups sugar for each cup rose water

Pour rose water into a saucepan and add sugar. Bring to a boil. Lower heat and let simmer until a syrup forms, stirring occasionally, about 12 minutes. Pour the syrup into a glass jar. Store at room temperature at least 1 week before serving. Refrigerate to store for a longer time.

LEMON-HONEY SYRUP

1 cup sugar   ½ lemon
1 cup water   2 tablespoons honey

Boil the sugar, water, and lemon for 15 minutes in a small saucepan. Remove the lemon and add the honey. Stir.

MAKES 1 GENEROUS CUP

HOREHOUND CANDY
(OLD-FASHIONED COUGH DROPS)

Marrubium vulgare, though native to Europe, Asia, and northern Africa, has been naturalized in many parts of the United States. An ancient herb, it was used as a cough remedy as far back as ancient Egypt and is one of the bitter herbs of Passover.

1¼ cups boiling water   2 cups sugar
1⅓ cups horehound leaves, packed   ⅛ teaspoon salt
⅓ cup light corn syrup

Butter a 9-inch-square pan. Pour the boiling water over the leaves and steep, covered, for 10 minutes. Strain, reserving the liquid, and discard the leaves. Transfer the horehound infusion to a saucepan. Stir in the corn syrup, sugar, and salt. Bring to a boil, and continue boiling until a candy thermometer measures 280 degrees, the soft-crack stage. Pour the candy into the buttered pan. Before it hardens, score it to mark the candy into ¾-inch squares. Break into squares when cool.

MAKES ABOUT 2 TO 3 DOZEN CANDIES

CARNATION CANDY

¼ cup firmly packed red or pink
    carnation petals
2 cups powdered sugar, or more as needed

1 egg white
Pinch of powdered cloves
1 cup shredded coconut (optional)

Place the carnation petals in a mortar and grind to a pulp with a pestle. Transfer to a bowl. Add the powdered sugar gradually; add the egg white. Stir, mixing thoroughly. Continue adding powdered sugar until a smooth, stiff fondant paste forms. Add the cloves and coconut, if desired. Blend well.

Put the paste into a pastry tube or zippered plastic bag with a tip cut off in one corner. Force the paste through the bag onto a sheet of waxed paper. Add a bit of chocolate on top, if desired. Let dry.

MAKES 2 TO 3 DOZEN CANDIES

CANDIED FENNEL OR CORIANDER SEEDS

Candied herb seeds, with their sweet-pungent taste, are served after a heavy meal for their supposed help in aiding digestion.

¾ cup fennel or coriander seeds
2 tablespoons sugar

1 tablespoon water
1/16 teaspoon baking soda

Toast the seeds lightly in a heavy skillet over medium heat. Transfer to a dish to cool. Bring the sugar and water to a boil in a small saucepan, stirring to dissolve the sugar. Boil for 1 minute to create a syrup. Remove from heat and add the herb seeds and then the baking soda, stirring rapidly to coat evenly. Cover a plate with waxed paper and pour the seeds onto it to cool. Shake the plate to separate the seeds. Store in a covered container. The seeds can be eaten as a snack, served with coffee after dinner, sprinkled on fruit compotes, or added to trail mixes.

MAKES ABOUT 1 CUP

CARAWAY AND FENNEL COOKIES

Herb seeds were one of the earliest flavors for cookies and confections.

1 tablespoon caraway seeds

2 cups unbleached all-purpose flour

2 teaspoons baking powder

2 teaspoons fennel seeds, ground

1 teaspoon salt

4 tablespoons unsalted butter or margarine,
    at room temperature

½ cup sugar

1 large egg

⅔ cup whole milk

1 teaspoon vanilla

1 teaspoon grated orange zest

Toast the caraway seeds in a heavy skillet over medium-high heat until fragrant, about 3 minutes. Transfer to a plate and let cool completely.

Combine the flour, baking powder, ground fennel seeds, and salt in a bowl. Beat the butter in a large bowl until pale; add the sugar and continue beating until light and fluffy. Stir in the egg, milk, vanilla, orange zest, and caraway seeds. Pour the milk mixture over the flour and mix into a dough. Divide the dough into 2 pieces. (The dough can be set aside for up to 1 week in the refrigerator or for up to 3 months in the freezer. Bring back to room temperature before rolling out.)

Preheat the oven to 375 degrees. Roll out 1 piece of the dough, dusting often with flour, until it is ⅛ inch thick. Using a 2-inch cookie cutter, cut out cookies and arrange them on an ungreased baking sheet. Continue with the remaining dough the same way. Finally, gather up the scraps, roll again, and cut into cookies.

Bake in the middle of the oven for 12 minutes, until golden. Cool on racks. The cookies can be stored at room temperature for up to 3 weeks in a covered container.

MAKES 4 DOZEN 2-INCH COOKIES

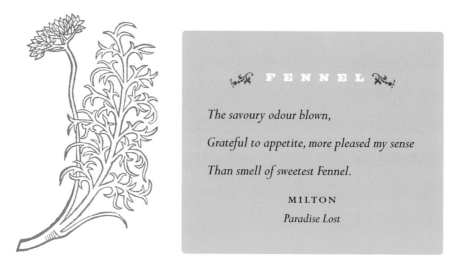

FENNEL

The savoury odour blown,

Grateful to appetite, more pleased my sense

Than smell of sweetest Fennel.

MILTON
Paradise Lost

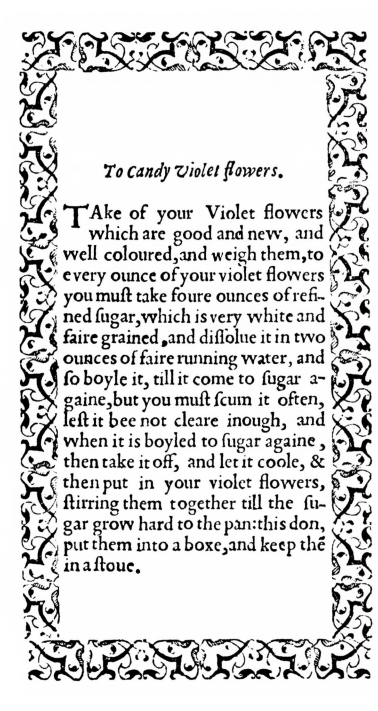

To Candy Violet flowers.

TAke of your Violet flowers which are good and new, and well coloured, and weigh them, to every ounce of your violet flowers you must take foure ounces of refined sugar, which is very white and faire grained, and dissolue it in two ounces of faire running water, and so boyle it, till it come to sugar againe, but you must scum it often, lest it bee not cleare inough, and when it is boyled to sugar againe, then take it off, and let it coole, & then put in your violet flowers, stirring them together till the sugar grow hard to the pan: this don, put them into a boxe, and keep thē in a stoue.

Take of your Violet flowers which are good and new, and well coloured, and weigh them, to every ounce of your violet flowers you must take foure ounces of refined sugar, which is very white and faire grained, and dissolue it in two ounces of faire running water, and so boyle it, till it come to sugar againe, but you must scum it often, lest it bee not cleare inough, and when it is boyled to sugar againe, then take it off, and let it coole, & then put in your violet flowers, stirring them together till the sugar grow hard to the pan: this don, put them into a boxe, and keep thē [them] in a stoue.

A Closet for Ladies and Gentlewomen,
1611 edition (first published in 1608)

The tiny, pocket-sized book from which this recipe is taken concentrated on two rather different kinds of instructions —how to make sweets (preserves, candies, syrups) and how to make medicines and salves. Alas, no recipe for the logical combination of these two skills, the sugar-coated pill, is included. Flowers were common ingredients in many recipes; one book claimed that "Conserue [medicine or confection made with part of a plant, preserved with sugar] of roses cōforteth [comforteth] the stomack the hart and all the bowels it mollifieth and softneth the bowels, and is good against blacke choller [choler, one of the four humours; biliousness] and melancholy. Conserue of white roses doth lose the belly more than the red."

ROSE- OR HERB-SCENTED MADELEINES

Ah, these light little cakes with the subtle flavor of roses or herbs would be perfect for an afternoon tea or just coffee for two with someone special on a rainy afternoon. Or, like Proust, they might conjure up your remembrance of things past . . . or hope for the future!

¾ cup unsalted butter
3 large eggs, brought to
 room temperature before using
⅔ cup (scant) granulated sugar

1 cup sifted cake flour
1 tablespoon rose water, or to taste
About ½ cup powdered sugar

Preheat the oven to 375°. Spray the madeleine mold pans with a corn oil cooking spray and set aside. Heat the butter gently and clarify it by skimming off milk solids, leaving only the clear liquid. This will reduce the amount somewhat. Set aside to cool. Using an electric mixer, in a medium-size bowl, beat the eggs and sugar until the mixture is quite frothy, pale yellow, and forms a single ribbon-like stream when the beaters are lifted from the bowl. Add the sifted flour, a third at a time, gently folding it in each time. Next, add the rose water, a little at a time to taste. If you have some fresh rose petals (minced), you may add them now. Fold these new ingredients in gently but completely.

Fill each madeleine mold about ⅛-inch from the top, as the batter will expand somewhat in baking. Place the pan in the preheated oven and bake until just golden brown about the edges, about 10 to 11 minutes. Remove each madeleine to a wire cake rack, top side down, and sprinkle with the sifted powdered sugar.

These madeleines are best eaten the same day they are made. They are sinfully light and delicious when still warm from the oven! They freeze well, if necessary. However, if you clarify the butter; pick, measure, and mince the roses or herbs; sift the flour; and measure the granulated sugar ahead of time, they then go together and bake so quickly, you might consider making and baking them at the last minute for very special guests!

VARIATION: Instead of rose water, use ½ cup minced fresh fragrant pink or red rose petals. Use only those you are certain are pesticide- and fungicide-free. Do not use roses from the florist. Or, try 1 tablespoon grated fresh lemon zest and 2 tablespoons finely chopped lemon balm, lemon thyme, or mint leaves, or 2 teaspoons grated fresh orange zest and 1 teaspoon finely chopped tarragon leaves, minced.

NOTE: Intensity of rose water varies widely, depending upon source. It can be purchased from cooking supply stores or from Middle Eastern delicatessens. I recommend you make your own from a rose in your garden whose scent you prefer. Roses do not all smell alike! See page 138 for directions.

MAKES 24 MADELEINES

CHAMPAGNE MINT SORBET

Festive and refreshing, this dessert was a hit at one of our recipe-tasting parties.

1 cup water
1 cup sugar
2 cups lightly packed fresh mint leaves
   and stems, coarsely chopped

3 tablespoons lemon juice
1 bottle chilled champagne,
   sparkling wine, or apple juice
¼ cup chopped fresh mint leaves

Combine the water, sugar, and the 2 cups of mint in a saucepan and bring to a boil. Lower heat, and simmer 5 minutes. Remove from heat and let steep 15 minutes. Strain and let cool completely.

Add the lemon juice, champagne, and remaining mint leaves; pour into a shallow dish. Freeze for several hours or overnight, until firm throughout, stirring occasionally.

SERVES 6 TO 8

LEMON TARRAGON SORBET

The combination of citrus with herbs appeals to everyone.

2½ cups water

1 cup sugar

1 cup lemon juice

1 tablespoon chopped fresh tarragon

1 tablespoon minced fresh lemon verbena

In a small saucepan, bring the water and sugar to a boil over high heat; stir to dissolve the sugar. Chill. Add the lemon juice, tarragon, and lemon verbena. Freeze in an ice cream maker according to the manufacturer's directions.

MAKES ABOUT 3 CUPS, 4 TO 6 SERVINGS

MARJORAM-INFUSED PEACH ICE CREAM

1 cup whole milk

¼ cup chopped marjoram leaves, removed from stems

2 cups diced ripe peaches, peeled and pitted

¼ cup orange liqueur

4 large eggs, separated

2 cups half-and-half or light cream

¾ cup sugar

> ## MARJORAM
>
> *Marjoram tea was drunk to treat head colds, coughing and lung problems, and diseases of the chest. It was also thought to help digestion of foods, especially meats, and relieved torments of the belly.*

Bring the milk to a boil in a small saucepan; remove from heat and add the marjoram. Cover and set aside to cool.

Combine the peaches with the liqueur in a medium bowl. Cover and set aside.

Beat the egg whites in a large bowl until soft peaks form. Set aside.

Combine the egg yolks, cream, and sugar in a medium saucepan and blend until smooth. Cook over medium heat, stirring constantly, until thickened, about 10 to 15 minutes. When ready, the custard should just coat the surface of a spoon. Remove immediately and beat the mixture into the egg whites. Let cool.

Strain the marjoram infusion and discard the marjoram leaves. Pour the infusion into the custard. Add the peaches and orange liqueur; mix well.

Pour into an ice cream maker and freeze according to the manufacturer's instructions. Or, pour into a 9 × 13 × 2-inch freezer-proof dish; cover and freeze until ready to serve. Allow 8 hours to freeze thoroughly.

MAKES 2 1/2 PINTS, 5 TO 6 SERVINGS

SWEET LAVENDER ICE CREAM

Dried lavender buds are somewhat sweeter than fresh because the small amount of menthol in lavender evaporates.

2 cups milk
2 tablespoons dried English
   lavender flower buds
1 cup sugar

2 egg yolks, beaten slightly
2 tablespoons minced crystallized ginger
1 teaspoon minced fresh orange zest
2 cups heavy cream, chilled

Heat the milk slowly until it simmers—just below boiling; bubbles will form around the edge of the pan. Remove from heat and add the lavender. Cover and let steep for about 15 minutes. Strain the milk through a cheesecloth-lined strainer.

While the milk is still warm, stir in the sugar until dissolved. Pour some of the milk into the egg yolks, then pour this mixture back into the milk. Return it to the saucepan, add the ginger and orange zest, and cook, stirring, over low heat until just below boiling. The mixture will thicken and coat the back of a spoon when it is ready, or it will reach 200 degrees on a candy thermometer.

Remove from heat; add the chilled cream. Mix well and refrigerate. When cold, place in the freezer, stirring occasionally, or process in an ice cream machine.

MAKES 1 QUART

EAST INDIAN ROSE PUDDING (RAVO)

Before vanilla was readily available, rose water was a popular flavoring for desserts.
Use a good-quality, not-too-strong rose water. Or make your own (page 138). Cream of wheat
may not seem appropriate for a dessert, yet people are always surprised that this tastes so good.

1 cup sliced almonds
2 tablespoons butter
¾ cup seedless raisins
4 cups milk
1 cup sugar

¼ cup cream of wheat
1 to 2 tablespoons rose water
½ teaspoon ground nutmeg
½ teaspoon ground cardamom

Sauté the almonds in butter in a medium skillet until golden. Add the raisins and cook lightly, until soft. Remove from heat and set aside.

Heat the milk and sugar in a saucepan. Add the cream of wheat and cook, stirring, until thickened. Remove from heat and add rose water to taste. Start with 1 tablespoon if the flavor is new to you. Add the nutmeg, cardamom, and all but ¼ cup of the almonds and raisins. Pour into a flat serving dish, and sprinkle the top with the reserved almonds and raisins. Serve hot or warm.

MAKES 4 TO 6 SERVINGS

Plate 353.

The Nutmeg.

Eliz. Blackwell delin. sculp et Pinx

1. unripe Fruit.
2. ripe Fruit.
3. Fruit open.
4. Shell with its Mace
5. Mace.

6. Shell.
7. Shell open.
8. Female Nutmeg.
9. Male Nutmeg.
10. Nutmeg open.

Nux
Moschata.

RUSSIAN ROSE CREAM

Use your own rose water (see page 138 for how to make it),
or you can buy it at most grocery or liquor stores.

1 cup light cream
¾ cup sugar
1½ teaspoons unflavored gelatin
1 tablespoon cold water

2 tablespoons
  rose water
1 cup sour cream
Fresh or frozen fruit

Heat the cream and sugar in the top of a double boiler until lukewarm. Soften the gelatin in the water; add to the cream mixture and stir until dissolved. Remove from heat and cool. Add the rose water. Beat the sour cream until it is smooth and fluffy; add to the cream mixture.

Pour into individual molds or a single 2-cup mold. Refrigerate 3 to 4 hours, until set. Unmold and serve with partially thawed fruit or fresh fruit.

MAKES 4 SERVINGS

> ## ROSE
>
> *The wine wherein dyed roses have been boyled, is good against the paine of the head, the eyes, the eares, the iawes or gummes, the bladder, the right gutte, and of the Mother or women's secretes, eyther powred or annoynted with a fether.*
>
> DODOENS

HERBED BAKED CUSTARD

Herbs and spices add subtle variety to custard, so feel free to experiment. Serve warm
or chilled, and enhance with a topping of fresh berries or any other fruit in season.

1½ cups milk
2 bay leaves
3 eggs, beaten

Pinch of salt
⅓ cup sugar

Preheat the oven to 325 degrees. Fill a large baking pan one quarter full with water and place in the oven. Heat the milk with the bay leaves to just below boiling. (A thin skin forms on the top, and bubbles will form at the edge of the pan.) Remove from heat and cover. Let steep for at least 15 minutes.

Remove the bay leaves and add the eggs, salt, and sugar; stir well. Pour into four 6-ounce custard cups or one 3½-cup baking dish. Place the cups in the baking pan filled with hot water. Bake 35 to 45 minutes for individual cups or 50 to 60 minutes for a single dish, until a knife inserted in the center comes out clean.

VARIATION: Use any of the following herbs instead of bay leaves: 2 tablespoons fresh sweet marjoram or 2 teaspoons dried; ¼ cup fresh lemon balm; 2 fresh allspice leaves; ¼ cup fresh cinnamon basil; 6 fresh lemon verbena leaves; ¼ teaspoon freshly ground nutmeg; ¼ cup fresh lemon basil. **MAKES 4 SERVINGS**

BASIL BERRIES

*The purple basil has a wonderful, vibrant look, with a fruity undertone, and the others
lend their particular nuances of flavor to the luscious ripe berries of summer.*

½ cup sugar

3 tablespoons cornstarch

½ teaspoon salt

2 cups sweet muscatel wine

4 cups blackberries

4 cups raspberries

1 cup fresh cinnamon, lemon,
 or anise basil sprigs, coarsely chopped

1 teaspoon lemon juice

2 teaspoons vanilla

Fresh basil leaves for garnish

BASIL

*In India basil is considered
a sacred plant, a passport to
paradise. A leaf of basil may
be placed on the breast of
a Hindu who is laid to rest.*

Whisk together the sugar, cornstarch, and salt in a large saucepan. Set aside.

In a small saucepan, simmer the wine and ½ cup of each berry. Drain in a sieve over a bowl, reserving the liquid. Transfer the cooked berries to a large bowl and stir in the remaining fresh berries.

Whisk the reserved hot liquid gradually into the sugar mixture until smooth. Stir in the basil. Bring to a boil, whisking; simmer for 3 minutes, stirring occasionally. Immediately pour the mixture through a sieve over the berries, discard the basil, and stir until well combined. Stir in the lemon juice and vanilla.

Divide into 6 or 8 individual bowls, cover and chill for at least 3 hours, or up to 3 days. Garnish with fresh basil leaves.

MAKES 6 TO 8 SERVINGS

PEAR TART WITH ANISE CREAM

Sprinkle the tart with anise seeds before serving, if you like.

3 large ripe Bartlett pears, peeled,
 halved, cored, and stemmed

Press-in Pastry

½ cup (¼ pound) cold butter
 or margarine, cut into cubes

1 (3-ounce) package cold cream cheese,
 cut into cubes

1 cup all-purpose flour

Anise Cream

⅓ cup sugar

2 tablespoons cornstarch

1 teaspoon anise seeds, crushed

2 cups half-and-half

2 egg yolks

To make the pastry, combine the butter and cream cheese with the flour in a food processor. Whirl until the mixture holds together. Press the dough evenly into the bottom and sides of an 11-inch tart pan with a removable bottom.

With a knife, decoratively score the round side of the pears. Lay the pears, flat side down, in a buttered 9 × 13-inch pan.

In a 375-degree oven, place the tart shell on a low rack; place the pears on the rack above. Bake until the pastry crust is golden and the pears turn brown, 20 to 30 minutes. Cool.

While the pastry and pears are baking, mix the sugar, cornstarch, and anise seeds in a small saucepan. Add the half-and-half. Stir over medium-high heat until boiling. Stir some of the sauce into the egg yolks; add yolks to the hot mixture and stir 1 minute. Use hot.

Pour the hot anise cream over the crust. Set the pears, round side up, in the cream. Let cool, cover lightly with waxed paper, and chill 3 hours, or overnight. Cut into wedges.

MAKES 6 TO 12 SERVINGS

ANISE

Anniseeds dissolves windiness,

belching and blasting of

the stomach and belly,

and helpeth their

griping and torments.

LANGHAM

CARAWAY APPLE TART

Caraway and apple go well together.

Crust
- 1 ½ cups all-purpose flour
- ½ cup (¼ pound) butter, cut into cubes
- 3 tablespoons vegetable shortening, chilled
- Pinch of salt
- 2 tablespoons sugar
- ⅓ cup cold water

Filling
- 3 ½ tablespoons sugar
- ¼ teaspoon vanilla
- ½ cup half-and-half or light cream
- 1 teaspoon caraway seeds
- 3 large apples, peeled, cored, and thickly sliced (3 cups)
- ⅛ teaspoon ground cinnamon

To make the crust, place the flour, butter, and shortening into a medium bowl. With your fingertips or a pastry blender, cut the butter and shortening into the flour. Do not overmix, or pastry will be tough. When blended, the mixture will resemble a coarse meal.

Dissolve the salt and sugar in the cold water. Add to the flour mixture and blend rapidly with a wooden spoon or spatula. Turn out onto a lightly floured surface and knead slightly. If the dough becomes sticky, dust lightly with flour. As soon as the dough softens, roll into a ball, wrap in waxed paper, and refrigerate. The dough should be refrigerated for at least 2 hours, or as long as several days.

Remove the dough from the refrigerator, unwrap it, and place on a lightly floured surface. Hit the dough in several places to soften it. Roll it out into a 14-inch circle. Transfer to an ungreased 11-inch tart pan with a removable bottom or a 10-inch pie pan. Do not prick the crust or allow tears or holes to remain unmended because liquids may leak through later.

Preheat the oven to 375 degrees. Combine 3 tablespoons sugar and the vanilla with the half-and-half; set aside to completely dissolve.

Sprinkle caraway seeds evenly over the raw crust. Arrange the apples in concentric circles inside the tart shell. Sprinkle with the remaining sugar and cinnamon. Bake for 25 to 30 minutes, until the apples are light brown. Lower the oven temperature to 350 degrees. Remove the tart from the oven; pour the half-and-half mixture over the apples. Return to the oven and bake 15 to 20 minutes longer.

✿ MAKE-AHEAD TIP: *The dough can be frozen for up to a week before rolling out. If it will be stored for longer than 1 day, wrap the dough in waxed paper or plastic wrap, and place in a zippered plastic bag to keep it from drying out. Freeze. To defrost, place in the refrigerator for at least 24 hours.*

MAKES 8 TO 10 SERVINGS

✤ CARAWAY ✤

Nay, you shall see my orchard, where,

in an arbour, we will eat a last year's

Pippin of my own graffing, with

a dish of Caraways, and so forth.

SHAKESPEARE
Henry IV, Part II

APPLE NIGELLA TART

*Available in Middle Eastern markets, nigella seeds are small, black, and crescent-shaped with
a lovely, haunting flavor. A major mail-order spice company sells it under the name of Charnuska.*

Crust
- 1 ½ cups all-purpose flour
- ½ cup (¼ pound) butter, cut into cubes
- 3 tablespoons vegetable shortening, chilled
- Pinch of salt
- 2 tablespoons sugar
- ⅓ cup cold water

Filling
- ½ cup milk
- ½ cup heavy cream
- ⅓ cup sugar
- 2 teaspoons nigella seeds
- 2 large apples, peeled, cored, and thickly sliced (2 cups)
- ½ tablespoon sugar

To make the crust, follow the directions for the Caraway Apple Tart crust on the facing page. Roll the dough out into a 9 × 14-inch rectangle. Transfer to an ungreased 8 × 12-inch rectangular tart pan. Do not prick the crust or allow tears or holes to remain unmended because liquids may leak through later.

Preheat the oven to 375 degrees. Combine the milk and cream. Stir in the ⅓ cup sugar until dissolved.

Sprinkle nigella seeds evenly over the crust. Arrange the apples in three rows, lengthwise, inside the tart shell. Sprinkle with the ½ tablespoon sugar. Bake for 25 to 30 minutes, until the apples are light brown. Lower the oven temperature to 350 degrees. Remove the tart from the oven; pour the milk mixture over the apples. Return to the oven and bake 15 to 20 minutes longer.

MAKES 8 TO 10 SERVINGS

APPLE ROSEMARY TARTE TATIN

Best eaten warm from the oven with a dollop of crème fraîche or a scoop of vanilla ice cream.

Crust

- 1½ cups all-purpose flour
- 2 tablespoons sugar
- ½ teaspoon kosher salt
- ¾ cup (6 ounces) cold unsalted butter, cut into cubes
- 2 egg yolks, beaten with 1 tablespoon water

Filling

- 1 cup sugar
- 10 large Granny Smith apples, peeled, quartered, and cored
- 2 tablespoons unsalted butter, melted
- 1½ tablespoons minced fresh rosemary

To make the crust, place the flour, sugar, and salt in a food processor and pulse just to combine. Add the butter and pulse until most of the butter is incorporated into the flour. Add the yolk mixture and pulse until mixture just begins to come together. Gather the dough into a ball, flatten into a disk, wrap in plastic, and refrigerate.

To make the filling, place the sugar in an 11-inch ovenproof skillet over medium-low heat. When the sugar begins to melt, stir until it melts completely and turns into a caramel-colored syrup. Be careful not to let the syrup burn. Remove from heat.

Toss the apples with the melted butter and rosemary. Arrange the apples in the skillet on top of the syrup in 2 layers, making concentric circles; put the first layer in core side down and the second layer core side up.

Place over medium heat and cover the skillet. Cook for 5 minutes. Uncover and cook for 10 minutes. Set aside to cool.

Preheat the oven to 350 degrees. Roll the dough out on a floured surface into a circle slightly larger than the skillet. Place the dough over the apples; fold in the extra dough, pressing it against the skillet to form a seal. Bake until the crust is lightly browned, about 30 minutes.

Let stand for 10 minutes. Quickly—but carefully—invert the skillet over a large plate or platter. Serve warm.

MAKES 8 SERVINGS

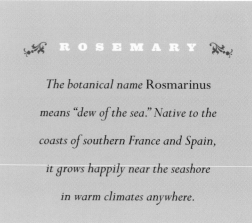

ROSEMARY

The botanical name Rosmarinus *means "dew of the sea." Native to the coasts of southern France and Spain, it grows happily near the seashore in warm climates anywhere.*

Ancient Egyptians and later Greeks, Romans, and Arabs cultivated anise. Fresh leaves may be used in salads, vegetables, and cooked dishes. Seeds and oil are used to flavor candy, confections, and curries, as well as many anise-flavored drinks such as Pernod, ouzo, rake, and arak. Native to southwestern Asia, northern Africa, and southeastern Europe and cultivated for more than two thousand years, anise has never been seen growing in the wild!

ANISE PECAN DESSERT CRÊPES

Whip up a batch of these crêpes in no time with a little practice.
Store between layers of waxed paper if they are made ahead of time.

1 ¼ cups milk
3 large eggs
3 tablespoons sugar
¼ teaspoon salt
1 cup all-purpose flour

4 tablespoons butter, melted
½ teaspoon baking powder
1 teaspoon anise seeds, crushed
¼ cup finely chopped pecans
15 pieces waxed paper, 8 to 10 inches wide

Combine the milk, eggs, sugar, salt, flour, 1 tablespoon butter, and baking powder in a blender; process 20 seconds. Scrape down the sides of the bowl and process again for another 20 seconds. Transfer to a container with a cover; stir in the anise seeds and pecans. Cover and refrigerate for at least 1 hour. (The batter can be kept in the refrigerator for up to 3 days. Stir well before using.)

Place a 6- to 7-inch skillet over medium heat. Brush the bottom of the skillet with a small amount of the remaining 3 tablespoons melted butter. Using a ¼-cup measure, pour a little less than ¼ cup of the batter into the skillet. Tilt the skillet to coat the bottom evenly. Cook until the top is set and the edges begin to turn golden brown, about 1 to 2 minutes. Turn the crêpe over and cook the underside.

Transfer to a waxed paper–covered plate. When cool, slide the crêpe off the plate—paper and all—to another plate, and later onto the stack of freshly made, cooled crêpes. Place a new piece of waxed paper on the original plate. Pour more batter into the skillet and cook until done. These crêpes can be served with many different fillings and sauces, including the following recipe.

MAKES 15 CRÊPES, 6 TO 7 INCHES

LEMON THYME POACHED PEACHES

1½ cups sugar
4¼ cups water
½ vanilla bean
5 whole cloves

4 (3-inch) sprigs fresh lemon thyme
Zest of ½ lemon
4 large ripe peaches, peeled and sliced
2 tablespoons cornstarch

Combine the sugar and 4 cups water over high heat in a medium saucepan, stirring to dissolve the sugar; bring to a boil. Add the vanilla bean, sliced in half lengthwise, along with the cloves, lemon thyme, and lemon zest. Simmer 10 minutes. Add the peaches and cook until they just begin to get soft, but not mushy. Lower the heat. Mix the cornstarch and remaining ¼ cup cold water until well blended. Add to the fruit mixture and cook, stirring until the mixture is clear and thick. Remove immediately from heat. When cool, pour into a container and cover. Can be kept covered in the refrigerator for several days.

To assemble with crêpes, remove the vanilla bean, cloves, and lemon thyme sprigs from the fruit. Place 1 crêpe on a plate. Pour ¼ cup fruit and syrup onto the crêpe. Fold the crêpe in half. Garnish with a dollop of crème fraîche, sour cream, or whipped cream and sprinkle with a few fresh lemon thyme leaves.

WHITBY NUNS' CAKE

Whitby was a monastery in Northumbria occupied by nuns and monks around 700 A.D.

1 cup (½ pound) butter, at room temperature
1½ cups sifted flour
¼ teaspoon baking soda
1½ cups sugar
1½ tablespoons lemon juice
1 teaspoon ground cinnamon
½ teaspoon ground coriander

1 tablespoon caraway seeds
1 teaspoon rose water
5 eggs, separated
⅛ teaspoon salt
1 teaspoon cream of tartar
Powdered sugar (optional)

Grease a 9-inch tube pan or a 9 × 5-inch loaf pan with 1 tablespoon of the butter. Dust with flour; remove excess. Put the flour, soda, and ¾ cup of the sugar in a bowl. Add the rest of the butter and mix in well with your fingers. Add the lemon juice, cinnamon, coriander, caraway seeds, and rose water. Add the egg yolks, one at a time, mixing with your fingers until well blended. In another bowl, beat the egg whites with salt until stiff but not dry. Gradually beat in the remaining sugar; add the cream of tartar. Add the first mixture and fold in with your hands or a rubber spatula until the whites are thoroughly mixed in.

Spoon into the pan and spread evenly with the back of a spoon. Shake the pan gently to remove any air bubbles. Bake at 325 degrees for 1 hour. Turn off the heat and let stand in the oven for 10 to 15 minutes. Loosen with a spatula and turn out onto a waxed paper–covered rack; cool. Dust with powdered sugar if desired. Store in an airtight container. MAKES 1 LOAF

CORNMEAL CAKE WITH SWEET ROSEMARY SYRUP AND RASPBERRIES

*A wonderful dessert for summer, when you want a light cake to serve
with fresh berries, and the rosemary syrup is good enough to eat with a spoon.*

Cake

½ cup (¼ pound) unsalted butter,
   at room temperature

1 cup sugar

1 cup yellow cornmeal

¾ cup all-purpose flour

1 teaspoon baking powder

¾ teaspoon salt

2 large eggs

1 large egg yolk

⅔ cup milk

Rosemary Syrup

1½ cups sugar

1½ cups water

1 cup fresh rosemary, chopped

2 tablespoons lemon juice

1 teaspoon vanilla

Accompaniments

Lightly sweetened whipped cream,
   sour cream, or mascarpone

2 half pints raspberries or
   sliced fresh white peaches

Preheat the oven to 350 degrees. Butter and flour an 8-inch round cake pan.

In a large mixing bowl, cream the butter and sugar until light and fluffy. Add the cornmeal, flour, baking powder, salt, eggs, egg yolk, and milk; beat on low speed until combined. Beat the batter on high speed until pale yellow, about 3 minutes.

Pour the batter into the prepared pan and bake in the middle of the oven 40 minutes, until a toothpick comes out with a few crumbs adhering.

While the cake is baking, simmer sugar, water, rosemary, and lemon juice in a small saucepan for 10 minutes. Remove from heat and strain through a sieve into a 2-cup measure; stir in the vanilla. Cool the syrup 30 minutes.

Cool the cake in the pan on a rack 10 minutes. Invert the cake onto a second rack. While the cake is still warm, gradually brush ⅓ cup syrup over it, allowing the syrup to soak in before adding more. Chill the remaining syrup in a small pitcher, covered. This syrup-soaked cake can be made 1 day ahead and kept wrapped in plastic wrap at room temperature.

Serve the cake, cut into wedges, with whipped cream, sour cream, or mascarpone, raspberries or peaches, and the remaining rosemary syrup.

MAKES 8 SERVINGS

CHOCOLATE-ORANGE CAKE
WITH MINT MARSHMALLOW ICING

2 cups all-purpose flour
1 teaspoon baking soda
Pinch of salt
1 cup (½ pound) unsalted butter,
    at room temperature
5 ounces unsweetened baking chocolate,
    coarsely chopped

1¾ cups strong-brewed coffee, hot
¼ cup orange liqueur
2 cups sugar
2 large eggs
1 teaspoon vanilla
Mint Marshmallow Icing (see recipe below)

Preheat the oven to 275 degrees. Grease two 8-inch round cake pans with shortening. Line the bottoms with waxed paper and grease the paper. Dust the pans with flour, tapping out the excess.

In a bowl, whisk together the flour, baking soda, and salt. In a large bowl, combine the butter, chocolate, coffee, and orange liqueur; stir occasionally until the chocolate and butter melt. Stir in the sugar until it dissolves and the mixture is completely cool. Add the flour mixture in 2 batches, whisking between additions. Whisk in the eggs and vanilla.

Divide the batter evenly between the 2 prepared pans and bake in the middle of the oven for 1 hour 15 minutes, until a toothpick inserted in the center of the cakes comes out clean. Let the cakes cool completely on a rack. Refrigerate for at least 6 hours or overnight.

To unmold the cakes, set the pans, one at a time, over a burner on low heat for 10 seconds. Run a blunt knife around the cakes to loosen, then invert them onto a rack. Remove the paper. Split each cake in half horizontally to make 4 layers.

Place 1 cake layer on a stiff cardboard round on a rack and spread with ½ cup icing. Repeat with the remaining cake layers and icing, ending with a plain cake layer. Pour the icing over the cake, spreading it around the top and sides with a metal spatula. Refrigerate briefly to set the icing.

MAKES ONE 8-INCH CAKE, 10 TO 12 SERVINGS

Mint Marshmallow Icing

1 cup boiling water
⅓ cup packed fresh mint leaves
2 egg whites

1½ cups sugar
¼ teaspoon cream of tartar
½ teaspoon vanilla

Make an infusion by pouring the boiling water over the mint leaves. Let steep, then strain. Combine the egg whites, sugar, ⅓ cup mint infusion, and cream of tartar in the top of a double boiler. Place over boiling water and beat until soft peaks form. Remove from heat. Fold in the vanilla. Beat until cool.

CHOCOLATE MINT MOUSSE
WITH CHOCOLATE MINT SAUCE

The cultivar 'Chocolate Mint' works especially well in this recipe, but you can also try spearmint, a cultivar called 'Mint the Best,' or peppermint for a sharper mint flavor.

½ cup boiling water
¼ cup coarsely chopped mint leaves,
    densely packed
2 ounces unsweetened chocolate
1 ounce bittersweet chocolate

3 egg whites
1 cup sugar
2 cups heavy cream
½ teaspoon vanilla
Whole mint leaves for garnish

Make an infusion by pouring the boiling water over the mint leaves. Cover and steep for 30 minutes. Strain the mint, pressing the leaves against the strainer. Place the infusion in the top of a double boiler. Add the chocolates and melt over hot water, stirring occasionally. Let cool.

Beat the egg whites until stiff but not dry. Add the sugar gradually to the whites, beating constantly. The meringue should be thick and glossy.

Whip the cream until soft peaks form. Fold the whipped cream, vanilla, and cooled melted chocolate mixture into the beaten egg whites.

At this point, you can divide the mousse into 8 to 10 individual dishes, or fill cream puffs (your own recipe or store bought) with the mousse. Either way, the cream can be placed in the freezer until ready to serve. Serve with Chocolate Mint Sauce (see recipe below) and garnish with mint leaves. **MAKES 8 TO 10 SERVINGS**

Chocolate Mint Sauce
    ¼ cup boiling water
    2 tablespoons coarsely chopped mint leaves
    9 ounces semisweet chocolate
    1½ ounces unsweetened chocolate
    1 tablespoon butter
    ½ cup milk

Pour the boiling water over the mint leaves; cover and let steep 30 minutes. Strain, pressing the leaves against the strainer. Melt the chocolates and butter in a double boiler over hot water. Stir in the milk and 2 tablespoons of the mint infusion. Stir until well blended. Serve warm.

MINT

Ovid once related how a very poor couple were visited by two guests. Despite their poverty, they wished to welcome their guests and make their home inviting. They gathered mint and rubbed their rustic table with the leaves until the fragrance so filled the room that their guests, none other than Zeus and Hermes, were delighted with their efforts. Immediately, their cottage was transformed into a temple and the couple never knew want or deprivation again.

Plate 294.

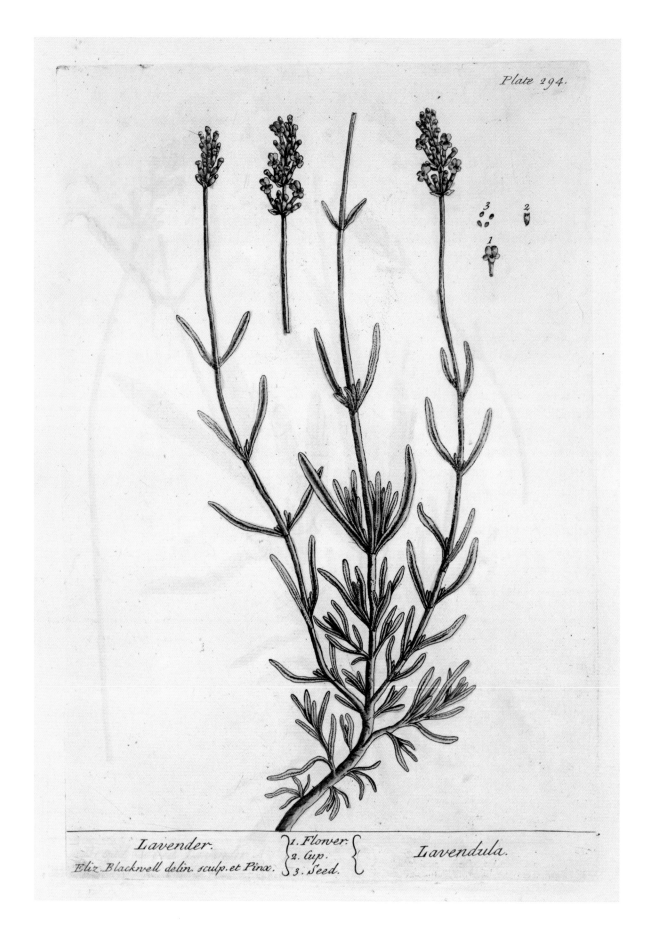

Lavender.

Eliz. Blackwell delin. sculp. et Pinx.

1. *Flower.*
2. *Cup.*
3. *Seed.*

Lavendula.

CHAPTER 11

Jams and Jellies

Savory jellies make fine companions to meat and poultry dishes. Brushed over chicken or ham before roasting or grilling, they add a sweet tartness, along with an herb flavor. Use sweet jams to glaze fruit pies, top a cream cheese base in tiny tarts, accompany scones at teatime, or add as a filling in holiday thumbprint cookies. Warm, sweet jams become a sauce for ice cream, custard, and bread pudding. Chilled, they can be used as a cake filling or in a trifle.

For details on how to process jams and jellies, refer to the instructions that come with commercial pectin.

TARRAGON FIG JAM

Figs are extremely perishable, so here's a fragrant jam to make
when you're blessed with more figs than you can eat at one time.

5 pounds fresh figs
6 cups sugar
¾ cup water
¼ cup lemon juice

1 tablespoon dried tarragon
4 inches of vanilla bean,
    cut into ¼-inch lengths

Cover the figs completely with boiling water. Let stand 10 minutes. Drain, stem, and chop the figs. Measure 2 quarts chopped figs.

Combine the figs, sugar, and water in a large pot. Bring to a boil slowly, stirring until the sugar dissolves. Cook rapidly until it reaches the gelling point, stirring frequently.

Add the lemon juice, tarragon, and vanilla bean; cook 1 minute.

Remove from heat. Skim the foam if necessary. Ladle into hot sterilized jars. Seal and process 15 minutes in a boiling water canner.

MAKES ABOUT 5 PINTS

SPICED PEACH JAM

Make this jam when your peach tree is overloaded or when peaches are on sale!

3 teaspoons whole allspice
1 tablespoon peeled and sliced
    fresh ginger (2 inches)
1 (4-inch) cinnamon stick, broken into pieces
4 cups peeled, pitted, and crushed peaches

½ cup water
¼ cup lemon juice
3 cups sugar

Place the allspice, ginger, and cinnamon in a cheesecloth bag. Tie with clean thread or twine.

Combine the peaches, spice bag, water, and lemon juice in a large pot. Cook gently 10 minutes. Add the sugar, stirring until dissolved. Return slowly to a boil. Cook about 15 minutes, stirring to prevent the mixture from sticking to the pan and burning. After the mixture reaches the gelling point, remove the spice bag.

Ladle the jam into hot sterilized jars, leaving ¼-inch headspace. Seal and process 15 minutes in a boiling water canner.

MAKES ABOUT 4 PINTS

GINGER

Queen Elizabeth I, knowing how popular gingerbread was in her time, hired a special baker who would create gingerbread men and women in the likenesses of her courtiers! The father of Peter the Great of Russia received many creations fashioned from gingerbread, including a large coat of arms of Moscow.

The botanical name Salvia *comes from the Latin word* salvere, *meaning to be saved. This referred to the amazing claims made for its powers to bring good health to mankind. In fact, an old Arab proverb asked, "How can a man die who has sage in his garden?"*

An interesting belief in rural England of years ago held that a family's fortunes were reflected in the prospering of a sage plant.

SAGE GRAPE CONSERVE

Use with plain cream cheese for a tea sandwich or spread on a toasted English muffin. Or, you can simply eat it with a spoon!

1 cup boiling water
13 fresh sage leaves, finely minced (or try
   two 4-inch sprigs fresh rosemary)
8 cups stemmed grapes, not all ripe (4 pounds)
5 cups sugar
1 cup seedless raisins
1 cup chopped walnuts
1 orange, seeded, chopped in a food processor

To make the sage infusion, pour water over 10 sage leaves. Cover and let stand 10 minutes; remove and discard the sage leaves.

Squeeze the insides of the grapes into a small saucepan. Put the skins in a large saucepan. Cook the pulp 30 minutes, until soft and mushy, adding a little of the sage infusion if necessary. Strain the pulp through a food mill to remove the seeds. Add the seeded pulp to the skins.

Cook the grapes 1 hour. Add the sugar and sage infusion; cook 20 minutes. Add the raisins, walnuts, chopped orange, and the last 3 sage leaves. Bring to a boil. Simmer gently 15 minutes, until thickened. Pour into hot sterilized jars and seal.

🌿 VARIATION: *To make Thyme Grape Conserve, follow the above recipe using thyme instead of sage. To make the thyme infusion, substitute 2 teaspoons dried thyme or 1 tablespoon fresh thyme for the 10 sage leaves. Substitute 1 teaspoon dried thyme leaves or 2 teaspoons fresh thyme leaves for the 3 sage leaves added toward the end of the recipe.*

MAKES 6 PINTS

LAVENDER PEACH CONSERVE

Drying the lavender buds releases the menthol flavors and retains the sweet lavender fragrance and flavor. Use this conserve plain on crackers or toast points, try it in thumbprint cookies, or spread it on crumpets or scones. Make sure to use only English lavender or lavandin cultivars, which are sold as Lavandula angustifolia *or* Lavandula × intermedia *hybrids.*

4 cups peeled, pitted, and crushed peaches
2 tablespoons lemon or orange juice
1½ cups sugar

½ tablespoon dried lavender buds
½ cup sliced almonds
1 teaspoon minced orange zest

Combine the peaches and lemon juice in a large pot. Bring to a boil and simmer gently 10 minutes. Add the sugar, lavender, almonds, and orange zest; return to a boil slowly, stirring to prevent sticking. Cook rapidly to the gelling point.

Remove from heat. Ladle hot jam into hot sterilized jars, leaving ¼-inch headspace. Seal and process 15 minutes in a boiling water canner.

MAKES ABOUT 4 1/2 PINTS

MINT JELLY

This mint jelly's delicate, fresh flavor goes well with lamb.

1½ cups firmly packed fresh
   mint leaves and stems
2¼ cups water
2 tablespoons lemon juice

A few drops of green food coloring
3½ cups sugar
½ bottle liquid pectin

Put the mint in a large saucepan and crush with the bottom of a glass. Add the water and bring quickly to a boil. Remove from heat, cover, and let stand 10 minutes.

Strain and measure 1⅔ cups of the mint infusion into a large saucepan. Add the lemon juice and food coloring. Stir in the sugar, place over high heat, and bring to a boil, stirring constantly.

Stir in the pectin; boil rapidly for 1 minute, stirring constantly. Remove from heat, skim off the foam with a spoon, and pour into hot sterilized jars. Seal.

MAKES 2 PINTS

As far as we know, French tarragon has been cultivated for only about five hundred years, a relative newcomer. However, what it lacks in heritage it makes up for in versatility and devotees to its hauntingly beautiful flavor. Like all herbs, it should be used with restraint. More is not necessarily better!

TARRAGON JELLY

One drop of green food coloring will tint this jelly a pale lime green; three to four drops will make it a darker and brighter green.

¼ cup fresh tarragon, or 3 tablespoons dried
2½ cups boiling water
¼ cup cider vinegar

1 (1¾-ounce) box pectin
4½ cups sugar
1 to 4 drops green food coloring

Place the tarragon and water in a bowl. Cover and let stand 15 minutes. Strain into a medium saucepan. Add the vinegar and pectin. Bring to a rapid boil over high heat. Stir in the sugar all at once. Bring to a full boil and cook for 1 minute, stirring constantly. Remove from heat and stir in the food coloring. Skim off the foam with a spoon. Pour the jelly into hot sterilized jars. Seal.

MAKES 1 1/2 PINTS

APPLE SAGE JELLY

Great with pork chops or roast chicken.

2½ cups sweet cider or apple juice
⅓ cup fresh sage, or 3 tablespoons dried
3¼ cups sugar

A few drops of yellow food coloring
½ cup liquid pectin

Bring ½ cup cider to a boil. Pour over the sage leaves. Cover and let stand 15 minutes. Strain through cheesecloth, adding water, if needed, to make ½ cup. Add the remaining cider and sugar; heat to boiling. Add enough food coloring to tint the mixture a pale yellow. Add the pectin, stirring constantly. Boil hard 1 minute. Remove from heat, skim, and pour into hot sterilized jars. Seal.

MAKES 3 PINTS

Plate 116.

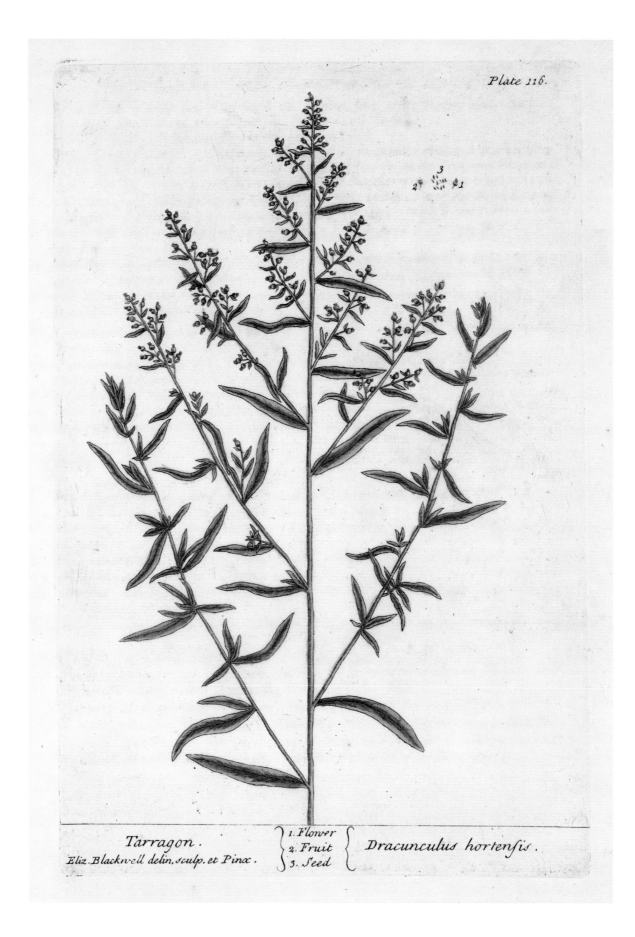

Tarragon.

Eliz. Blackwell delin. sculp. et Pinx.

1. Flower
2. Fruit
3. Seed

Dracunculus hortensis.

THYME GRAPE JELLY

Use lemon thyme, caraway thyme, or any other thyme variety.

½ cup boiling water
3 (4-inch) sprigs fresh thyme, or 1 tablespoon dried
1½ cups grape juice
3 cups sugar
½ cup liquid pectin

Pour water over the thyme; cover and let stand 5 minutes. Strain through a fine cheesecloth. Add enough water to make ½ cup.

Add the grape juice and sugar; heat to boiling in a small saucepan. Add the pectin, stirring constantly. Boil hard for 30 seconds. Remove from heat, skim, and pour into hot sterilized jars. Seal.

✻ VARIATION: *Use ¼ cup fresh red or cinnamon basil, or 1 tablespoon dried, to replace the thyme.*

MAKES 2 PINTS

> ❧ **THYME** ❧
>
> *Thyme was used not only in the kitchen but also as a strewing herb. Fresh branches were placed on the floor so that as they were walked on a pleasant fragrance was emitted to mask other less pleasant smells in the home or gathering place.*

ROSELLE JELLY

Roselle calyces contain a natural pectin, much like that of apples or grapes, so this jelly does not need any commercial pectin.

2 quarts whole roselle fruit
3 cups water

2¼ cups sugar

Wash and drain the fresh roselle fruit. Place in a saucepan and add water to almost cover the fruit. Place over medium-high heat and bring to a boil. Simmer gently for about 10 minutes, until the fruit is soft. Strain through a cheesecloth-lined colander, squeezing out as much liquid as possible.

Measure the juice. Add enough water to make 3 cups. Return to the pan and add the sugar. Bring to a boil again and cook, stirring occasionally, until the gelling point is reached, or a candy thermometer reaches 222 degrees.

Ladle the hot jelly into hot sterilized jars, leaving ¼-inch headspace. Adjust the caps and seal.

MAKES 1 1/2 PINTS

CANDIED CITRUS PEELS WITH TARRAGON SUGAR

Enjoy candied citrus peels by themselves or as a garnish for desserts such as cheesecake.

1 orange

2 lemons

2 cups sugar, plus ½ cup for coating the peels

2 cups water

2 tablespoons lemon juice

2 tablespoons chopped fresh tarragon

Cut the orange and lemons in half and juice them. Using a small spoon, separate the membrane from the pith, leaving the peel intact. Slice the peels into rings or strips ¼ inch wide.

Bring 6 cups water to a boil in a medium saucepan. Blanch the peels in boiling water for 10 minutes. Meanwhile, bring another 6 cups water to a boil in a second saucepan. Using a slotted spoon, transfer the peels to the second saucepan, discarding the water and cleaning the first saucepan. Boil 10 minutes, then repeat this process with 2 more changes of water. This processing will remove the bitterness from the peels.

Bring the 2 cups sugar, water, and lemon juice to a boil in a medium saucepan over low heat. Add the citrus peels and simmer gently until they are translucent, about 2 hours. The longer the peels cook, the more sugar they will soak up. Keep the heat very low and be careful not to let the sugar mixture burn. Add equal amounts of sugar and water to the saucepan as necessary to keep the peels covered.

Line a counter with waxed paper or plastic wrap. Place a wire rack over the paper. Place the citrus peels on the rack; let dry overnight.

Combine ½ cup sugar with tarragon in a food processor. Toss the citrus peels in the tarragon sugar, coating them thoroughly. Serve or store in a covered container at room temperature for up to 2 weeks.

🌿 VARIATION: *Use fresh mint instead of tarragon. Dip the citrus peels halfway in melted chocolate; let cool before serving.*

MAKES ABOUT 40 PIECES

🌿 TARRAGON 🌿

Tarragon is good in Sallads with Lettuce as

Rocket is, and is sharpe and salt inough of

it selfe, without the helpe of vineger and salt.

LANGHAM

PICKLED NASTURTIUM SEEDS (IMITATION CAPERS)

Use pickled nasturtium seeds as you would capers: in salads, pasta, or with vegetable and meat dishes. Gather the seeds while still green and plump, then rinse and let dry.

2 cups nasturtium seeds
1 whole clove
1 whole allspice berry
¼ teaspoon mace

1 tablespoon olive oil
½ teaspoon grated horseradish
2 cups distilled vinegar
¼ teaspoon salt

Place the nasturtium seeds, clove, allspice, mace, olive oil, and horseradish in a medium bowl. Heat the vinegar and salt until just below boiling. Pour the vinegar over the spices and seeds. Cover and let marinate for 24 hours. Refrigerate in a covered container. Can be kept in the refrigerator for up to 1 month.

MAKES ABOUT 2 CUPS

Plate 36

Borrage

Eliz. Blackwell delin sculp et Pinx.

1 *Flower*
2 *Calix*
3 *Seed*

Borago

CHAPTER 12

Beverages

Herb Teas

In colonial times, when tea was expensive because of the taxes levied on it by the British, American house-wives used native plants to make their tea. After the Boston Tea Party, these herbal beverages were called "Liberty Teas." The most popular herb was bee balm or *Monarda,* several species of which are native to the East Coast, but other herbs for tea included sweet goldenrod, mint, clover, chamomile, lemon balm, sage, sweet marjoram, and thyme.

Today's herb teas present a variety of flavors. Some taste better with honey added as a sweetener. As a general rule, use 1 tablespoon of a fresh herb or 1 teaspoon dried for every 6 ounces (¾ cup) of water. Pour boiling water over the herb leaves and cover to retain the flavors, let steep 5 to 10 minutes, then taste. Longer steeping intensifies the flavors but, in some cases, can make the tea bitter. Adjust the amount of herbs and water to your own taste, and add honey if desired.

Or try anise, fennel, caraway, and dill seeds, which were once made into teas for colicky babies because they were thought to reduce flatulence. Other herbs used to make a tisane or herb tea are Mexican tarragon (*Tagetes lucida*), pineapple sage, lemon balm, and what many consider to be the best of all, lemon verbena (*Aloysia triphylla*). Lemon thyme in hot cider is also a nice autumn drink.

Cold Beverages

Herbs combine so well with fruit flavors that the addition of herbs enhances many nonalcoholic, cold beverages. To vary basic lemonade, consider adding sprigs of mint, lemon balm, lemon verbena, pineapple sage, sweet woodruff, or slices of ginger root.

In earlier times, herbs frequently flavored ale, beer, and wine. For instance, a common name for carnation was "sops-in-wine," indicating its use in flavoring white wine. In medieval times, borage was thought to impart courage, so those departing on a journey received a glass of wine with a sprig of borage in it.

For a festive touch at a dinner party, try placing a fresh carnation or garden pink in a wine glass or a single perfect leaf of either lemon balm or lemon verbena in a glass of sherry. A blue borage flower in either white wine or sherry will impart a memorable flavor and also cause your guests to comment.

MINT SYRUP

Mix with bourbon to make a mint julep, add to vodka or gin for a meteor,
or pour a teaspoon into a cup of steaming hot cocoa.

1 cup plus 1 tablespoon sugar
1 cup water
1 cup mint sprigs, loosely packed

Heat 1 cup of the sugar with the water in a small saucepan; stir until the sugar dissolves. Mash the mint and the remaining 1 tablespoon of sugar in a bowl with a wooden spoon for about 15 seconds. Pour the sugar water over the mint and let it steep for 1 minute. Strain through cheesecloth and chill.

MAKES 1 1/3 CUPS

MINTED LEMONADE SYRUP

Your guests will beg you for the secret of this lemonade: it is the vanilla and mint.

2 cups sugar
1 cup water
⅛ teaspoon salt
Zest of 2 lemons

2-inch vanilla bean
2 (3-inch) sprigs mint,
  or ¼ cup fresh mint leaves
1 cup lemon juice

Combine the sugar, water, salt, lemon zest, vanilla bean, and mint in a small saucepan. Boil 5 minutes. Strain and cool; add the lemon juice. To serve, add ⅓ cup syrup to 1 glass water; stir.

MAKES ABOUT 3 CUPS OF SYRUP

ROSELLE JUICE

For a lovely color and fine taste, add this juice to your next batch of lemonade.

2 quarts whole fresh roselle fruit
3 cups water

Pick the fruit when the calyces are swollen and reddish. Wash and place in a large saucepan. Add water to cover the fruit halfway. Bring to a boil over medium-high heat and simmer until the fruit is soft, about 7 to 10 minutes. Pierce with a fork to test. Remove from heat and strain the juice through two thicknesses of cheesecloth. The juice can be made stronger or milder by adjusting the amount of water used.

Sweeten to taste and serve over ice cubes or combine with other fruit juices or carbonated lemon beverages.

SWEET YOGURT MINT COOLER

Very refreshing on a hot summer day.

3 cups water
1 cup packed fresh mint leaves

3 cups plain yogurt
3 teaspoons sugar

To make the mint infusion, boil the water and pour over the mint leaves. Cover and let cool. Strain and refrigerate until needed.

For 1 glass of this sweet cooler, combine 1 cup yogurt with ½ cup mint infusion. Stir well. Add 1 teaspoon sugar, or sweeten to taste.

MAKES ABOUT 3 CUPS

HERBED YOGURT DRINK

*This beverage is based on a traditional Persian recipe for "dugh." Try using
1 teaspoon each of the fresh herbs and rose petals if you have them available.*

1 cup plain yogurt
1 ½ cups water or club soda
½ teaspoon salt
¼ teaspoon dried savory

¼ tablespoon dried chervil
¼ teaspoon dried mint, powdered
¼ teaspoon fragrant rose petals, dried and
  powdered (or a few drops of rose water)

Put the yogurt into a blender and blend until smooth. Add the water, salt, savory, chervil, mint, and rose petals; blend until frothy. Pour over ice and serve.

MAKES 2 TO 3 SERVINGS

PIMM'S CUP
WITH BORAGE

Enjoy this traditional English beverage on a summer day.

In a glass pitcher, measure for each person 1 measure Pimm's No. 1, 1 glass fizzy lemonade, a sprig of borage, and some borage flowers. Make as much as you like, using the same proportions and adding slices of cucumber and orange and lots of ice cubes.

BORAGE

"Ego borago gaudia semper ago"

was an old adage which means,

"I borage always bring courage."

Sprigs of Borage are of known

virtue to revive the hypochondriac

and cheer the hard student.

EVELYN

Plate 32

Water Mint

Eliz. Blackwell delin. sculp. et Pinx.

{ 1 *Flower*
{ 2 *Cup*
{ 3 *Seed*

Mentha aquatica
Sisymbrium

MAY WINE PUNCH

½ ounce dried woodruff
4 bottles dry white wine
1 pint fresh strawberries
1 bottle champagne
1 large jigger Benedictine

2 large jiggers cognac
1 cup sugar
1 pint mineral water
6 sprigs fresh woodruff
Ice in a bowl

Place the dried woodruff in a wide-mouthed jar; pour 1 bottle wine over it and steep 8 hours.

Halve the strawberries. Chill all of the liquids thoroughly. Do not place the ice in the punch; keep the punch chilled by placing a container of ice in the center of the punch bowl.

Pour the rest of the white wine, champagne, Benedictine, and cognac into the punch bowl. Dissolve the sugar in mineral water; add to the punch and stir. Add the strawberries and fresh sprigs of woodruff. Serve in chilled punch cups.

NOTE: *Use any good, dry white wine such as Riesling Rhine or a very dry Sauterne.*

MAKES 12 GENEROUS SERVINGS

HIPPOCRAS

A modern version of a mulled wine that was popular in medieval Europe.

2 small bottles white wine
1 ⅓ cups brown sugar
¾ cup minced fresh marjoram
2 peppercorns
3 slices lemon
1 teaspoon cinnamon
2 bottles lemon-lime carbonated soda, chilled
Crushed ice

Mix the wine, brown sugar, marjoram, peppercorns, lemon, and cinnamon in a pitcher. Let stand 4 hours. Strain and chill. Add the chilled soda right before serving over ice.

SERVES 12

WOODRUFF

In Germany it is customary to celebrate the first of May with a **Maibowle.** *Fresh sprigs of sweet woodruff are steeped in Rhine wine for several hours, then strained out. Fresh woodland strawberries may be added to the punch bowl or to the individual punch cups for a most delightful beverage with which to toast the coming of spring!*

MINTED WINE PUNCH

A surprising combination featuring anise and cinnamon.

1 large bottle white wine (Rhine or Riesling)
1 tablespoon fresh mint leaves
½ teaspoon anise seed
1 (2-inch) cinnamon stick

4 ounces grenadine syrup
White grapes, 2 cinnamon sticks,
    and pomegranate seeds for garnish

Chill the wine 4 hours. Crush or finely chop the mint leaves, anise, and cinnamon. In a small saucepan, mix herbs with 3 tablespoons water and the grenadine syrup. Cook over low heat 10 minutes, stirring frequently. Let stand 1 to 4 hours. When ready, strain and stir into the wine until the syrup dissolves. Pour into an iced punch bowl. Float white grapes on top, along with 2 cinnamon sticks and pomegranate seeds.

SERVES 4 TO 6

SPICED ROSELLE PUNCH

1 quart roselle juice
¾ cup sugar
16 allspice berries
10 whole cloves
1 (4-inch) cinnamon stick
¼ cup orange juice
1½ tablespoons lemon juice
½ cup rum (optional)

Prepare the roselle juice using either of the methods described in the recipes on pages 173 and 174. Place in a saucepan, add the sugar, allspice, cloves, and cinnamon, and bring to a boil; simmer 10 minutes. Strain. Just before serving, add the fruit juices and rum. Serve hot or cold.

Plate 317. *Flower Gentle. Amaranthus*

1. The Stalks grow to be three Foot high, the Leaves are a bright Green tinctured with Red, and the Flowers Red.
2. It is sown in Gardens, and flowers in July.
3. The Flowers are accounted cooling, drying and restringent, and from their Colour are supposed to be good to stop Bleedings and Fluxes of all Kinds.
4. Greek, Ἀμάρανθος. Latin, *Flos Amoris.* Spanish, Italian, *Amaranto.* French, *Passe Velours.* German, *Sammat Blum.* Dutch,

---

Plate 318. *Winter Savory. Satureia durior.*

1. It grows about eight Inches high, the Leaves are a grass Green, and the Flowers a pale Red.
2. It is planted in Gardens, and flowers in June and July.
3. This Plant is esteem'd heating, drying and carminative, good to expell Wind from the Stomach and Bowels, ease the Asthma and Affections of the Breast, open Obstructions of the Womb, and promote the Menses. This Plant is more used in the Kitchen than the Garden Savory.
4. Greek, Θύμβρα. Latin, *Thymbra.* Spanish, *Coriella.* French, German, *Saturon.* Dutch, Italian,

---

Plate 319. *Sweet Marjoram. Majorana.*

1. The Stalks grow about a Foot high, the Leaves are a light grass Green, and the Flowers white.
2. It is sown in Gardens, and flowers in July.
3. It is accounted good for all Distempers of the Head and Nerves, and opens Obstructions of the Liver and Spleen, & brings down the Catamenia. Outwardly it is used in Sweet Bags & Powders, and is an Ingredient in cephalic Snuffs.
4. Greek, Σάμψυκον, κ̀ Ἀμάρακον. Latin, *Sampsuchus & Amaracus.* Spanish, *Majorana.* Italian, *Majorana.* French, *Marjolaine.* German, *Meyeran.* Dutch,

---

Plate 320. *Rupture Wort. Herniaria.*

1. The Stalks grow about a Span long, the Leaves are a grass Green, and the Flowers a yellow Green.
2. It grows in Sandy Ground and flowers in July.
3. It is accounted cooling, drying and binding, and a Specific for Ruptures of all Kinds. Some commend it as good for the Stone, in the Kidneys, and Bladder.
4. Greek, Πολύγονον μικρον. Latin, *Polygonum minus.* Spanish, *Corriola menor.* Italian, *Correggiola minore.* French, *Correggiole.* German, *Beygrass.* Dutch,

No. 80.

Text from A Curious Herbal
by Elizabeth Blackwell, 1737

Growing, Harvesting, Drying, and Storing Herbs

Lack of space is never a reason for not growing herbs. An individual plant of chives, garlic chives, parsley, chervil, sweet marjoram, basil, savory, thyme, or common sage can occupy a space in a garden of less than eighteen inches square.

You can incorporate many herbs into most landscaping schemes. Much depends upon the climate, but if the following plants grow in your area, you can work them into a general landscape. *Laurus nobilis,* or bay laurel, makes a handsome large shrub or tree depending upon how it is shaped as it grows and does very well in containers, enabling it to be grown in places colder than zones 8 to 10 if it is brought indoors in winter. Determined northern gardeners have been known to coddle lemon verbena and rosemary in the same way. Fennel works in a perennial border along with lavender, angelica, lemon balm, lovage, pinks, violets, anise hyssop, and daylilies. The attractive and colorful flowers of many annual plants fit in anywhere. Dill, anise, calendula, borage, bread-seed poppies, nasturtiums, arugula, and cilantro/coriander enhance the beauty of the garden as well as the buffet table.

Most herbs do well in containers because good drainage, a basic requirement for success in growing herbs, is sometimes easier to achieve in a container or raised bed when the local soil is heavy and mostly clay. Use good commercial potting soil to ensure no contamination of harmful pathogens found in local garden soil. Most herbs require full sun, though in the hot, dry, southwestern part of the country many can handle only four to six hours of sun. Overwatering, whether in the ground or in a container, should be avoided.

Storing Fresh Herbs after Harvest

Many of the recipes in this book call for fresh herbs, and they can be harvested anytime as needed. If you need to purchase fresh herbs, keep them fresh until use by rinsing them in tepid water, removing blackened or damaged leaves, and recutting the stems. Place the herbs in a jar of fresh water. Basil *must* and other herbs *can* be kept on the kitchen counter. Parsley, dill, and chervil do well in a somewhat cooler environment, but a plastic bag should be placed over the herbs in the jar to reduce the drying effects of the fan in a frost-free refrigerator, and change the water in the jar every day or two. Do not be surprised if mint and basil send out roots! You may choose to keep a few rooted stems to plant in a pot or in your garden. Tarragon, chives, arugula, and other greens can be kept much like lettuce, wrapped in a clean tea towel, dampened by the moisture still clinging to the leaves after rinsing. Finally, borage and other edible flowers are best kept in a Ziploc bag.

Harvesting and Drying Herbs at Home

Dry your own herbs to use in winter or to give as gifts. During the drying process, some flavor or fragrance is lost along with the moisture that evaporates, so select the moment of most intense flavor concentration to compensate. Most herbs have the highest concentration of their characteristic flavoring compounds just before the plant begins to flower. Much of the energy manufactured by the plant goes into flower and seed production. Therefore, it is best to harvest leaves just before or when you see flower buds forming. The exception to this rule is French tarragon, a sterile sport that never flowers. Summer or early fall, when it is lush and robust, is the time to harvest French tarragon.

Plants release their fragrant oils during the day as the sun warms them. If you wait until late in the day, much of that day's production may have evaporated. However, during daylight hours leaves photosynthesize and produce the aromatic oils that we want to use. All of this boils down to mid- to late morning as the optimum time for harvest, or, as the old formula went, "when the dew has dried from the leaves in your garden."

Dry any of the following herbs easily at home with excellent results: basil, dill, French tarragon, lovage leaves, marjoram, mint, oregano, rosemary, sage, thyme, and woodruff.

When cutting the stems, do not cut the plant back more than one-third to one-half or you can send it into shock. You want it to survive and produce more leaves to use fresh during the growing season. Gather the stems, rinse them in cool water, pat them dry with clean tea towels, and lay them in a single layer in a clean, flat basket. Raise the basket a few inches from the surface of the shelf or table where you will set it to dry. Place it in a well-ventilated room, out of the direct sun. If you have no flat baskets, use your extra oven rack covered with a clean tea towel for this. Depending upon the weather and the moisture content of the herb, the drying time will vary from four days to two weeks, but you will know by feeling the leaves when they are thoroughly dry.

Now comes the fun part. Place a length of wax paper on a table in front of you. Remove the stems from the basket and, running your hands back along the stems from top to bottom, strip the leaves from the stems. Save the stems to tie up with paper ribbon in little bundles to throw on the BBQ or into the fireplace.

Store the leaves in small airtight glass jars, label with the name of the herb and the date of harvest, and store the jars in a cupboard away from heat and light. Creative packaging will delight your friends with your thoughtful gift from your garden!

Herb Chart

WITH REFERENCES TO HERBS AND SPICES
GROWN IN THE HUNTINGTON HERB GARDEN

Name of Herb	Description of Plant	Cultivation Notes	Culinary Uses	Comments
Allspice *Pimenta dioica*	A tropical tree that grows from 30 to 50 feet in its native habitat. Small berries are produced that, when dried, give us allspice. The lovely aromatic leaves can be used in cooking.	This native to the Caribbean Islands can be grown only outdoors in part shade in the mildest parts of Southern California and Florida. Elsewhere it can be grown as a houseplant, given bright diffused light, average amounts of water, and moderate humidity.	The berries available commercially whole or ground are used in Jamaica jerk marinades, smoked and pickled foods, ground meat dishes, fruit desserts, and puddings. Use the leaves as you would bay leaves to impart flavor to custards, sauces, marinades, and tea.	The berries lose flavor if left to ripen and dry on the tree. Unripe green berries are gathered and allowed to dry. Although it hasn't berried yet, an allspice plant is thriving in the Huntington Herb Garden.
Anise Seed *Pimpinella anisum*	Annual plant to 12 inches. White flowers.	Sun. Average water.	Mild licorice flavor. Use in breads, cookies, or confections. Interesting when sprinkled on cooked carrots, beets, cabbage, asparagus, or baked apples.	The plant frequently sold as "Sweet Anise" in grocery stores is actually fennel, not anise!
Arugula *Eruca vesicaria*	Annual that reseeds readily. 18 to 20 inches.	Sun or part shade. Average water. Cut back frequently to renew tender young leaves. If allowed to flower, it will reseed readily.	Fresh young leaves are a wonderful addition to salads. Also use instead of lettuce in chicken or luncheon meat sandwiches. Flowers are milder but still tasty.	Older leaves get tougher and bitter, so cut back frequently to renew fresh young leaves.

Name of Herb	Description of Plant	Cultivation Notes	Culinary Uses	Comments
Basil *Ocimum basilicum* cultivars	Annual herb. 12 to 24 inches tall. Space 15 inches apart.	Plant in May when soil is warm or whenever tomatoes are planted locally. Sun or part shade in hot areas. Ample water. Remove flowers to prolong life.	Especially good with tomatoes. Use also with fish, chicken, vegetables, pasta, mushroom, egg dishes, and salads. Also slivered onto soups at the last minute. Use fresh or dried.	Many kinds to grow and use include lemon basil, cinnamon basil, licorice basil, and red-leaf basil.
Bay Leaves *Laurus nobilis*	An evergreen shrub or tree that grows slowly from 10 to 30 feet in height, 5 to 15 feet in width.	A very forgiving plant, it can take full sun or part shade, and much or little water once established. It must have good drainage, however. Does very well in a container and can be pruned regularly to an appropriate size. In colder climates it can be brought indoors in winter.	True bay leaves, sold sometimes as Greek or Turkish bay, have a mild, almost sweet, flavor. Some commercial brands sell bay leaves from the California Bay tree, *Umbellularia californica*. They are very pungent and less desirable. All bay leaves are used in dishes that require long, slow cooking to release their flavor.	Because the leaves remain stiff and brittle even after cooking, they are not to be ingested. Remove the leaves before serving.
Borage *Borago officinalis*	An annual herb that grows to 3 feet. It will reseed nicely in the garden.	Almost a weed, but a beautiful one, it grows in sun or half sun, average water, and almost any soil.	The beautiful blue flowers have a cucumber flavor. They are delightful in salads, frozen in ice cubes, floated on chilled summer soups, or as a garnish. Use only the blue flower; pinch off the attached brown seeds and green calyx.	For a simple hors d'oeuvre, spread a cracker or slice of baguette with an herb butter and garnish with a borage flower.
Capers *Capparis spinosa*	A small deciduous shrub, it grows slowly to 4 feet tall, spreading to 5 feet. In summer it produces both foliage and bright white flowers with brilliant purple stamens.	This can be difficult to grow even in sunny Southern California, but it is worth the attempt. It must have perfect drainage. It would rather be growing out of an ancient aqueduct wall in Spain or Italy. Give it also full sun and average water.	The buds have a somewhat bitter taste that is enhanced by the salty brine in which they are preserved. Therefore, they are used to add a burst of pungent flavor to sauces, salads, and other composed dishes. They add a little perk to many appetizers and sandwiches as well.	The unopened buds are harvested each day in the early morning, sorted, and pickled in brine. The expense is due to this labor-intensive procedure. In specialty markets, you can also find caper fruit, which is just that, the fruit that forms after the flowers are spent.

Name of Herb	Description of Plant	Cultivation Notes	Culinary Uses	Comments
Caraway Seed *Carum carvi*	Annual from 15 to 18 inches. Handsome ferny leaves and white flowers. It may reseed but is not invasive.	Sun or part shade. Average water.	Pungent, peppery flavor with a hint of citrus, caraway is used in breads and pastries, cheese and noodle dishes, soups, stews, goulash, some vegetables, coleslaw, and sauerkraut. It is an old companion to fresh apples and apple desserts.	Caraway is a great favorite in Germany, Austria, and other Northern European countries, where even the root is cooked and eaten like carrots and turnips.
Chervil *Anthriscus cerefolium*	Annual. In Southern California it is best grown in fall and winter. Elsewhere it is a summer plant. 12 inches.	Part shade in hot areas, sun elsewhere. Ample water. Grow 6 or 8 plants together and/or sow crops 2 to 3 weeks apart to ensure plenty of young leaves.	Delicately flavored. Use in light sauces, soups, or egg dishes. Chop in salads. Add at last minute to broth. Use fresh only.	An ingredient of fines herbes along with chives, tarragon, and parsley.
Chives *Allium schoenprasum*	Perennial to 15 inches. Pink-lavender flowers are both edible and handsome.	Sun. Average water. Cut back to the ground to renew when tattered. Very easy to grow in a pot in the window.	One of the most important herbs to grow. Widely used. Use fresh leaves or flowers in dips, sauces, soups, salads, vegetables, fish, pasta, mushroom, and egg dishes.	A basic herb to grow at home so its fresh leaves are always available.
Cilantro *or* **Coriander** *Coriandrum sativum*	Annual. In Southern California it grows best in fall and winter. Summer herb elsewhere. It bolts or goes to seed quickly in hot weather.	Sun along coast, part shade inland. Ample water. Use young leaves as cilantro. Leaves become bitter when it flowers. Seeds are the spice coriander.	The seed, coriander, is used whole or dried in curries, spice mixtures, breads, and pastries. It flavors pickles, gin, and corned beef. It is also used extensively to make sausages, luncheon meats, cheese, fish, and chicken dishes. Sugar-coated seeds were an early form of candy and were called comfits. The fresh young leaves are cilantro and are used in salads, salsas, and Asian and Mexican cuisine.	Because they are rather woody, the seeds are usually ground before using. However, they are used whole in cooking corned beef, stews, and sausages. To bring out more aroma and flavor of the seeds, toast them lightly over medium heat in a non-stick skillet.

Name of Herb	Description of Plant	Cultivation Notes	Culinary Uses	Comments
Dill *Anethum graveolens*	Annual best grown in fall and winter in Southern California. Lacy foliage and yellow flower are quite lovely in the garden.	Sow seed in several places for best results. Sun or part shade. Ample water. Provide staking for tall-growing varieties.	Use fresh or dried leaves and seed. Or freeze the leaves to retain their fresh flavor. Leaves and seed are used to flavor breads, meats, fish, sauces, salads, and vegetables.	Yellow dill flowers are also pretty in bouquets.
Fennel *Foeniculum vulgare*	A hardy perennial to 3 feet. It dies down in winter and sends up fresh new shoots each spring. Yellow flowers are very decorative and appealing either in a bouquet or as a garnish.	Its long taproot may make it difficult to remove if you change your mind about growing it. The bronze form is particularly attractive in the garden. Sun and average amounts of water are all it needs to thrive. It will reseed.	Fennel seeds are used in many herb and spice mixtures, most notably in herbes de Provence. They flavor sweet Italian sausage, are wonderful in fish sauces and soups, and pair up well with pork and chicken. They also are used in breads and pastries. The fresh, ferny leaves make an attractive base on which to place grilled chicken or fish as it is brought to the table.	Strong licorice flavor is not to everyone's liking. An acquired taste for some, it soon becomes a favorite flavor. Florence fennel (*Foeniculum vulgare azoricum*) is the source of the fleshy stems that, sliced thin, are used much as celery.
Garlic *Allium sativum*	Annual to 2 feet. There are several cultivars with varying strenghts of flavor. Easy to grow by dividing cloves from fresh store-bought garlic.	Sun, average water, and loose soil. In Southern California, it is best planted in October for harvest when leaves turn yellow the following summer.	One of the most popular and widespread herbs. Its use goes back to ancient times. Not only the bulb is edible. Snip the tender young leaves and use their delicate flavor as you would chives. Roast a whole bulb and enjoy its sweet mild flavor in an herb rub or simply on toast.	Be careful when sautéing garlic that it does not burn, for then it will become strong and bitter.
Garlic Chives *Allium tuberosum*	Perennial from 18 to 24 inches. White flowers in clusters are decorative in the garden and they are edible.	Sun. Average water. Cut back to renew. It will reseed. Easy to grow in containers.	Use fresh leaves or flowers in sauces, soups, salads, fish, and egg dishes. Separate flowers into individual florets before sprinkling on cream cheese or salads.	Usually not available in markets, so it is best to grow your own.
Ginger *Zingiber officinale*	A tropical perennial plant to about 3 feet. It is best grown as an annual.	Sunny, warm, or part shade with ample water in rich, loose soil. Purchase a fresh young "hand" of ginger at the market and plant it in the garden in May.	Fresh ginger root is quite different in flavor from dried powdered ginger. Both are important flavorings for many kinds of food. Crystallized ginger makes a nice thing to nibble on instead of a heavy dessert after a rich meal.	Unleavened, honey-sweetened cakes flavored with ginger originated on the island of Rhodes about 2400 B.C. The Romans brought ginger to all parts of the empire.

Name of Herb	Description of Plant	Cultivation Notes	Culinary Uses	Comments
Horseradish *Armoracia rusticana*	Hardy perennial related to radishes and cabbage. Plant grows from 2 to 3 feet. Thick, fleshy root should be harvested each year to be used fresh or dried. Plant 1 or 2 lateral roots for the following year.	Plant in a sunny, but cool, location in rich, moist soil free of rocks and pebbles. May become invasive if not harvested regularly. Can be grown in a deep pot. Harvest large taproot at end of season. Scrub and slice thinly to dry. Store in glass container. Grate as needed.	Although it has been cultivated for thousands of years, its use in cooking goes back only a few hundred years. Horseradish is used mostly fresh. The grated root is mixed with vinegar and a little salt and sugar. It is best used in small quantities.	One of the bitter herbs of the Jewish Passover, the first young leaves in spring may be used sparingly in salads. The grated fresh root was applied as a poultice to aching joints or inhaled to clear sinuses.
Lavender *Lavandula angustifolia*	Bushy perennials to 3 feet tall and 3 to 5 feet wide bloom mostly in summer. The flower buds can be harvested and dried for later use.	Give full sun and excellent drainage. Thorough but infrequent water is best to prevent attack by soil-borne fungi. Though perennial, it is best to start with new plants every 3 to 5 years to maintain vigor.	Lavender flavor is an acquired taste. Though used in the south of France and as an ingredient of herbes de Provence, some people need to be introduced to it in very mildly flavored ways. Go easy at first. Use it in beverages, lamb and meat dishes, stews, desserts, or fruit dishes.	Many of the kinds of lavender have strong fragrances and flavors of menthol. Therefore, only the flowers of English lavender or of "lavandin" should be used in the kitchen.
Lemon Balm *Melissa officinalis*	Perennial. 12 to 18 inches and spreading.	Sun or light shade. Average water.	Fresh leaves used for sauces, custards, tea, or cold beverages.	Leaves can be rubbed on a wooden picnic table to allow the lemon oil to be absorbed.
Lemon Grass *Cymbopogon citratus*	Perennial grass growing 3 to 4 feet tall. Grown only in frost-free gardens outdoors.	Give full sun, ample water. Cut back in late spring or early summer for new supply of fresh young leaves. Grow in a pot in colder areas to take indoors in winter.	Important ingredient in Southeast Asian cooking. Like the other lemon-scented herbs, it can be used to flavor sauces, custards, and beverages. Use lower 6 inches, including the bulb, for soups. Use the top tougher leaves for tea or as a stirrer in cold drinks.	Cut back all leaves to the ground in late spring to renew the plant and obtain fresh tender shoots for culinary uses.
Lemon Verbena *Aloysia triphylla*	Small tree or large shrub. Deciduous and frost-tender.	In warm areas grow outdoors in full sun. Give ample water during growing season. Grow in containers in colder areas. Bring indoors in winter.	Sweet, lemon-flavored leaves are wonderful when used fresh in sauces or beverages. Good with custards, desserts, fish, and vegetables.	When dried, the leaves retain their lovely fragrance and are most useful in potpourris.

Name of Herb	Description of Plant	Cultivation Notes	Culinary Uses	Comments
Lovage *Levisticum officinale*	A hardy, deciduous perennial that can grow from 4 to 6 feet. It grows wild in the south of Europe.	In most areas it prefers full sun. In the hot, dry Southwest it prefers part shade. Rich soil. Average to ample water.	Strong celery flavor. Use fresh leaves, stems, or seeds in soups, stews, salads, salad dressings, vegetables, or turkey stuffing. The leaves and stalks retain their flavor longer than celery in long slow cooking. Seeds also go well with cabbage, potato, and cheese dishes.	Lovage seed was used as a digestive and to relieve flatulence after a heavy meal, and an infusion of lovage leaves was also used as a gargle and mouthwash.
Marjoram *Origanum majorana*	A half-hardy and short-lived perennial treated as an annual in many parts of the country. 12 to 18 inches high. Plant 9 inches apart for a nice border.	Full sun, average water. Trim frequently for longer life. Replant every 3 years as it does exhaust itself when grown as a perennial.	Slightly sweet, slightly floral, but warm and aromatic, its delicate complex flavor is best enjoyed when used fresh near the end of the cooking process. Also good in marinades, in salads, with fresh vegetables, and in mushroom, cheese, pasta, and egg dishes.	Home-dried sweet marjoram has more flavor than commercial. Harvest when flower buds form "knots" along the stem.
Mint *Mentha* sp.	A hardy perennial, it grows 18 to 24 inches.	Full sun to part shade. Ample water. Because of its invasive roots, mint is best grown in a container. Another perennial to replant every 3 to 4 years to maintain its vigor.	Mint is best used fresh, though it can be used dried. Its pungent, cooling flavor sparks up beverages, desserts, jellies, salads, and sauces. Try it in small amounts in marinades, ground meat dishes, and fruit soups as well.	This herb is used in small amounts and wonderful to have available for whenever you need it.
Nasturtiums *Tropaeolum majus*	A tender perennial grown as an annual in most areas of the country. Some forms are vining and need support; others have been hybridized for compact, bushy form. Gaily colored flowers appeal to children and adults alike.	Sun in most areas, but part shade in the hot Southwest. Well-drained sandy soil and average water is all it needs to shine.	Both leaves and flowers have a sprightly, peppery taste, though the flowers, being milder, appeal to most people. Remove the stamen and stuff with a filling or toss the flower petals in a salad.	Though easy to grow, they do not ship well, so it is best to grow your own for consumption when desired.

Name of Herb	Description of Plant	Cultivation Notes	Culinary Uses	Comments
Nigella *Nigella sativa*	Annual. 12 to 18 inches. Small, white flowers. Not to be confused with its very pretty cousin, *Nigella damascena,* whose beautiful flowers enliven many cottage gardens.	This annual herb is easily grown from seed. The seed is frequently sold in Middle Eastern markets and can be sown and grown much like dill and poppy seed.	Bright peppery taste with a hint of citrus. Use in cheese dishes, fruit desserts, and baked goods and pastries.	Nigella is an ancient herb/spice and is sold under several names, including "Black Cumin," "Roman Coriander," "Russian Caraway," and "Charnuska." Yet, sadly, it is little known and used today.
Oregano Several different plants yield commercial oregano. Grow *Origanum vulgare* ssp. *hirtum* at home.	Perennial. 1 to 2 feet and spreading.	Sun. Average water. Good drainage.	Strong flavor. Use sparingly. Good in Italian and Mexican foods. Used in tomato dishes, especially sauces, beans, beef, chicken, vegetables, sausage, and other meat dishes.	*Origanum onites* and *Origanum syriacum* are other European oreganos. The tender *Poliomintha longiflora* and *Lippia graveolens* are used in Mexico and are grown indoors in colder areas of the United States.
Parsley, Curly and Flat *Petroselinum crispum, Petroselinum crispum* var. *neapolitanum*	Annual best planted in fall and winter in Southern California. Needs more shade and water if grown in summer.	Sun or part shade. Average water. Good edging for a garden.	Use fresh leaves. Flat parsley has stronger flavor, but both have a somewhat sweet, fresh taste. Use in sauces, soups, fish, poultry, or meat dishes, and vegetables.	One of the most popular medieval herbs for sauces, soups, and relishes.
Pinks/Carnations *Dianthus* sp.	Like roses, there are many different kinds to choose from. Annuals or perennials. Choose the kind with the fragrance or flavor you like best.	Full sun, average water, and perfect drainage make *Dianthus* easy to grow. Use only home-grown, chemical-free flowers, not flowers from a florist.	Use the flower petals in desserts and in beverages where the sweet, clove-like flavor is compatible. Sprinkle the petals in a salad or use them as a garnish for open-faced sandwiches, cakes, or fruit tarts.	Carnations used to be called "sops-in-wine." To surprise and delight your guests, float a flower in a wine glass or punch bowl.
Rose *Rosa* species or cultivars	The taste of the rose will mimic its scent, so choose one that pleases you. Choose also a disease-resistant variety to eliminate the need for fungicides.	Roses like a minimum of 6 hours sun and at least an inch of water per week. Do not use fungicides or pesticides.	Rose water is used in many Middle Eastern dishes and is available in ethnic markets or delicatessens. Fresh roses or rose petals make attractive garnishes for many party dishes.	Smell commercial rose water before you buy it. Some are too strong or smell like perfume. Homemade is best and easy to do.

Name of Herb	Description of Plant	Cultivation Notes	Culinary Uses	Comments
Roselle *Hibiscus sabdariffa*	A bushy annual that grows from 3 to 4 feet tall and 3 feet wide. It is grown mostly in tropical or sub-tropical areas in summer.	Plant when the soil warms up in May or June. It needs much heat to develop flowers and fruit. Average to ample water.	It is the calyces, not the flowers, that are harvested and used fresh, if possible, or dried. The flavor is fruity and tart, like cranberries. It also gives its ruby-red color to the dishes or beverages in which it is used.	Travelers to Mexico or the Caribbean will find it used under the names "Roselle" or "Jamaican Sorrel," and it is also used in Red Zinger tea.
Rosemary *Rosmarinus officinalis,* many cultivars	Upright or trailing perennial or shrub. 2 to 6 feet.	Give full sun, good drainage, average to less water. Being tender, it is best grown in containers and brought indoors in winter in colder climates.	Strong flavor. Use leaves fresh or dried but don't overdo it. Very good in Mediterranean dishes. Also good with vegetables, lamb, chicken, or beef, bread, potatoes, game, stews, and soups.	A small branch of rosemary can be used to brush on BBQ sauce while grilling meat.
Saffron *Crocus sativus*	An autumn-flowering bulb whose bright orange stigmas are harvested and dried. Saffron bulbs are sold in many bulb catalogues.	Plant bulbs in rich, well-drained, sandy soil. Leaves appear after flowers and should be left on until brown, then cut off at the base. May be grown in pots in cold areas.	Saffron is another acquired taste for many. It is best to use it subtly at first until you get used to it.	About 200,000 flowers yield a pound of saffron, accounting for its high cost. Buy only threads of saffron, not ground saffron, which may be easily adulterated.
Sage *Salvia officinalis* cvs.	Perennial, short-lived. 18 to 24 inches.	Full sun, well-drained soil. Average to less water.	Strong flavor. Use fresh or dried with meat, poultry, bread, stuffings, soups, stews, vegetables, and tea.	Try sage tea made with boiling water (or apple juice) poured over 2 to 3 leaves and sweetened to taste with honey.
Salad Burnet *Poterium sanguisorba*	Short-lived perennial with clumping habit. Leaves rise to about 8 to 10 inches. Flower stalks may reach 18 inches, but are best removed to prevent reseeding. Burnet makes an attractive edging for an herb or vegetable garden.	Full sun, average water. Any soil. Cut back to ground in spring to renew plant with tender young leaves. May reseed.	Tender young leaves have a cucumber flavor and are used fresh in salads or as a garnish. They are appealing sprinkled on cucumber bisque.	According to Turner, 1562, "Some do hold that the juice . . . taketh freckles and spots out of the face. The virtue of this herb is so great against all venom and poison, that the root only, holden in a man's mouth, defendeth him wonderfully against the poison of the pestilence, as men of good experience do testify."

Name of Herb	Description of Plant	Cultivation Notes	Culinary Uses	Comments
Savory, Winter *Satureja montana* **Savory, Summer** *Satureja hortensis*	Winter savory is a small, bushy herb growing from 12 to 18 inches. Summer savory is an annual that is rather straggly in the garden but worth growing for its fine flavor.	Full sun, good drainage, and average amounts of water.	Because winter savory is quite pungent, it is best used in hearty dishes. Its German name, *bohnekraut*, reflects its time-honored use in flavoring bean dishes. Use it also, in small amounts, to season stews, meats, marinades, stuffings, and vegetables. Summer savory is a much milder version.	Though the flavor is strong, it is best used near the end of cooking. Fresh savory is best to use, but it can be dried by harvesting it just before it blooms.
Sorrel *Rumex acetosa,* *Rumex scutatus*	Common garden sorrel is a perennial plant that grows in great clumps to a height of 18 to 24 inches. It is very productive with an abundance of leaves. Many people prefer the true French sorrel (*Rumex scutatus*), only 1 to 2 feet tall. Though less productive with much smaller leaves, it has a sharper, more lemony flavor.	Full sun or part shade. Average to ample water. Cut back occasionally to renew and produce tender young leaves.	Sorrel soup simply made with a good chicken stock and served with warm crusty bread makes a marvelous light meal. Tender sorrel leaves of both kinds can be used instead of lettuce for variety in sandwiches. It can also be cooked like spinach, made into sauces, or added to salads.	John Evelyn wrote that sorrel imparted "so grateful a quickness to the salad that it should never be left out."
Spearmint *Mentha spicata*	Perennial, 18 to 24 inches and spreading. May be invasive. Best planted in a container. The cultivar 'Mint the Best' has a very pleasant flavor.	Sun or part shade. Average to ample water.	Use fresh or dried leaves with tea or other beverages, desserts, sauces, salads, soups, and jellies.	There are several kinds of mints, including spearmint and peppermint, to choose from. Select one whose fragrance or flavor you find most appealing.
Sweet Herb of Paraguay *Stevia rebaudiana*	Perennial treated as an annual. Grows 12 to 18 inches.	Sun or part shade. Average water. Grow in sheltered location.	Leaves are extremely sweet but have no aftertaste. Make an infusion of the leaves and use to sweeten beverages or other fresh or cooked, not baked, foods.	Used in Japan and other countries as an artificial sweetener for soft drinks, but much more needs to be learned of its uses.

Name of Herb	Description of Plant	Cultivation Notes	Culinary Uses	Comments
Tarragon, French *Artemesia dracunculus* 'Sativa'	Deciduous, perennial herb. 12 to 18 inches. Start with young plants because French tarragon does not flower and set seed.	Sun or part shade. Average water. Very easy to grow.	Superb taste reminiscent of licorice or anise mixed with parsley. Use sparingly for haunting and alluring flavor in sauces. Wonderful used fresh or dried with poultry, meat, fish, and vegetables. Mince a few fresh leaves in salads.	Harvest leaves in early fall to dry for winter use.
Tarragon, Mexican *Tagetes lucida*	Grown as an annual in colder areas and as a perennial in warm areas. 3 to 4 feet tall and as wide with cheerful golden yellow flowers in autumn.	Sun. Average water. Any soil. Can be grown in a container.	Somewhat stronger in flavor than French tarragon, otherwise quite similar. Use as you would French tarragon but in smaller amounts. Also makes a nice tea.	Leaves retain flavor and should be harvested before fall bloom.
Thyme *Thymus vulgaris* cvs.	Perennial. Height varies with cultivar.	Sun. Good drainage. Average to less water.	Use with meat, poultry, fish, vegetables, sauces, soups, and stews. Lemon thyme is nice with dessert sauces.	Many kinds of thyme are worth growing, including lemon thyme, French thyme, and caraway thyme.
Turmeric *Curcuma domestica*	A tender tropical perennial plant that grows to about 3 to 4 feet. Treat as an annual in colder areas.	Sun and average water with well-drained soil. Part shade in hot, dry areas might be best.	The rhizome or knobby root is the part used. Dried and powdered, it is readily available in markets. Used fresh, it has a pungent, distinctive flavor. Used dried, its flavor is quite mild and is valuable mostly for the golden color it provides.	This gives the bright gold color to both commercial curries and to some prepared mustards.
Woodruff *Galium odoratum*	A hardy perennial that grows to 12 inches. It makes a lovely ground cover under trees.	Woodruff prefers shady, moist situations.	The leaves may be used fresh or dried to make May wine. They contain coumarin, which has the scent and flavor of vanilla, and is sometimes used as an adulterant for vanilla extract. The main use of sweet woodruff is in beverages or sweet custard desserts.	The leaves retain their fragrance when dried and are lovely set in a small crystal bowl to scent a room.

Herb Sources

The information on this list was current at the time of publication. Telephone numbers and web addresses are subject to change, and we regret any inconvenience you may experience in reaching an enterprise listed here.

Abundant Life Seed Foundation
P.O. Box 772
Port Townsend, WA 98368
360-385-7192 [F] 360-385-7455
www.abundantlifeseed.org
Free catalog offers a variety of unusual herb and vegetable seeds, as well as a book on related topics.

W. Altee Burpee & Co.
300 Park Ave.
Warminster, PA 18991-0001
800-888-1447 [F] 800-487-5530
www.burpee.com
Free color catalog lists the most popular herb, vegetable, and flower seeds, along with onion and garlic bulb sets.

Companion Plants
7247 N. Coolville Ridge Rd.
Athens, OH 45701
740-592-4643
www.companionplants.com

Comstock, Ferre & Co.
263 Main St.
Wethersfield, CT 06109
800-733-3773
www.comstockferre.com
Online catalog features an extensive offering of seeds.

The Cook's Garden
P.O. Box 5010
Hodges, SC 29653-5010
800-457-9703 [F] 800-457-9705
www.cooksgarden.com
Fine source of many mail-order herb and vegetable seeds, books, and garden supplies. Catalog is $1.00.

Flowery Branch Seed Co.
P.O. Box 1330
Flowery Branch, GA 30542
404-536-8380 [F] 404-532-7825
Descriptive catalog ($2.00) lists herb seeds available by mail order.

Glasshouse Works
Church St.
Stewart, OH 45778-0097
800-837-2142 [F] 740-662-2120
www.glasshouseworks.com/pageone.html
Source of hard-to-find herb plants
and garden statuary. Free catalog.

Goodwin Creek Gardens
P.O. Box 83
Williams, OR 97544
800-846-7359 [F] 541-846-7357
www.goodwincreekgardens.com
Fine selection of herbs, other seeds, and plants. Home and
garden gifts, books, bath essentials, and bulk dried herbs.

The Gourmet Gardener
12287 117th Dr.
Live Oak, FL 32060
888-404-GROW [F] 407-650-2691
www.gourmetgardener.com
Hundreds of culinary herbs and gourmet vegetables,
gardening books and supplies, and gifts.

The Great American Spice Co.
P.O. Box 80068
Fort Wayne, IN 46898
888-502-8058 [F] 260-420-8117
www.americanspice.com
Order free catalog online, or shop online
for dried herbs and spices.

Herban Garden
5002 Second St.
Fallbrook, CA 92028-9790
760-723-2967
Retail and wholesale herbs at nursery.

Herb Products Co.
11012 Magnolia Blvd.
P.O. Box 898
North Hollywood, CA 91603-0898
800-877-3104 [F] 818-508-6567
www.herbproducts.com
Free catalog for mail order of dried herbs
and spices, as well as books on herbal topics.

Herb Society of America
9019 Kirtland Chardon Rd.
Kirtland, OH 44094
440-256-0514 [F] 440-256-0514
www.herbsociety.org
Dedicated to promoting the knowledge and use
of herbs through educational programs, research,
and community activities. Membership includes seed
exchange, publications, and library (via mail order).

J. L. Hudson, Seedsman
Star Route 2, Box 337
La Honda, CA 94020
www.jlhudsonseeds.net
Free catalog of different herbs
and other seeds. Quaint seed lore.

Johnny's Selected Seeds
184 Foss Hill Rd.
Albion, ME 04910
207-437-9294
www.johnnyseeds.com/catalog/index.html
Free catalog lists herb seeds available by mail order.

Logee's Greenhouses, Ltd.
141 North St.
Danielson, CT 06239
888-330-8038 [F] 888-774-9932
www.logees.com/store
Unusual and hard-to-find herbs and ornamental
plants available by mail order or at nursery.

Misty Ridge Herb Farm
P.O. Box 126
Mesick, MI 49668
231-885-2290
www.herbplantsonline.com
Online catalog.

Morningsun Herb Farm
6137 Pleasants Valley Rd.
Vacaville, CA 95688
707-451-9406
www.morningsunherbfarm.com
Online catalog.

Mountain Valley Growers, Inc.
38325 Pepperweed Rd.
Squaw Valley, CA 93675
559-338-2775 [F] 559-338-0075
www.mountainvalleygrowers.com
Great selection of organically grown herb plants by mail order only. Online catalog and free printed catalog.

Mulberry Creek Farms
3312 Bogart Rd.
Huron, OH 44839
419-433-6126
www.mulberrycreek.com/index.html
Offers organically grown herbs in small pots.

Native Seed Search/SEARCH
526 N. 4th St.
Tucson, AZ 85705
520-622-5561
www.nativeseeds.org
Mail order or retail at nursery. Specializing in heirloom and domestic varieties of herb and vegetable seed, plus Native American baskets and crafts, foods, and related publications.

Nature's Herb Co.
1010 46th St.
Emeryville, CA 94608
510-601-0700 [F] 510-601-0726
Free catalog. Mail-order source of herbs, spices, teas, and related products.

Nichols Garden Nursery
1190 Old Salem Rd. NE
Albany, OR 97321-4580
800-422-3985
www.nicholsgardennursery.com
Free mail-order catalog. Herb plants and seeds, dried herbs and teas, books, and home-brew and winemaking supplies.

Park Seed Company
1 Parkton Ave.
Greenwood, SC 29647-0001
800-845-3369 [F] 864-941-4206
www.parkseed.com
Free color catalog lists the most popular herb and vegetable seeds, some plants and garden supplies. Mail order.

Penzeys, Ltd.
19300 W. Janacek Ct.
Brookfield, WI 53045
800-741-7787 [F] 262-785-7678
www.penzeys.com
Free informative color catalog. Excellent mail-order source of dried herbs and spices.

Pinetree Garden Seeds
P.O. Box 300
New Gloucester, ME 04260
207-926-3400 [F] 888-527-3337
www.superseeds.com
Informative catalog listing herb and vegetable seeds. Bulbs and plants available by mail order, along with garden supplies, gifts, and books.

Renee's Garden Seeds
7389 W. Zayante Rd.
Felton, CA 95018
888-880-7228
www.reneesgarden.com
Excellent selection of kitchen, garden herb,
gourmet vegetable, and heirloom flower seeds
available online and at retail garden stores.

Richter's Herb Specialists
Goodwood, Ontario
Canada L0C 1A0
905-640-6677 [F] 905-640-6641
www.richters.com
Informative catalog. Mail order or visit nursery. All kinds
of herb plants and seeds, books, videos, and garden supplies.

Rosland Farm
NC82 at US13
Godwin, NC 28344-9712
Color catalog is $3.00. Wide variety of herb plants,
gifts, books, and kitchen accessories.

Sandy Mush Herb Nursery
316 Surrett Cove Rd.
Leicester, NC 28748-5517
828-683-2014 [F] 828-683-2014
www.brwm.org/sandymushherbs
Informative catalog listing unusual herbs
available by mail order.

San Francisco Herb Co.
250 14th St.
San Francisco, CA 94103
800-227-4530 [F] 415-861-4440
www.sfherb.com
Free brochure listing dried herbs and spices, blends,
essential oils, teas, baking, and food flavors by mail order.

Santa Barbara Heirloom Seedling Nursery
P.O. Box 4235
Santa Barbara, CA 93140
805-968-5444 [F] 805-562-1248
www.heirloom.com
Seedling plants and related products by mail.

John Scheeper's Kitchen Garden Seeds
23 Tulip Dr.
Bantam, CT 06750
860-567-6086
www.kitchengardenseeds.com
Online catalog.

Seeds of Change
P.O. Box 15700
Santa Fe, NM 87506
888-762-7333
store.yahoo.com/seedsofchange/index.html
Free mail-order catalog.

Shepherd's Garden Seeds
White Flower Farm
30 Irene St.
Torrington, CT 06790
800-503-9624 [F] 860-482-0532
www.whiteflowerfarm.com
Informative catalog for sale of herb, gourmet
vegetable, and heirloom flower seeds,
as well as cooking and gardening supplies.

R. H. Shumway's
P.O. Box 1
Graniteville, SC 29829-0001
803-663-9771
www.rhshumway.com
Free catalog.

Southern Exposure Seed Exchange
P.O. Box 460
Mineral, VA 23117
540-894-9480 [F] 540-894-9481
www.southernexposure.com
Online catalog or printed catalog ($2.00).

Spices Etc.
P.O. Box 2088
Savannah, GA 31402-2088
800-827-6373 [F] 800-827-0145
www.spicesetc.com
Online catalog describes dried herbs for sale by mail.

Sunnybrook Farms Nursery
P.O. Box 6
9448 Mayfield Rd.
Chesterland, OH 44026
440-729-7232 [F] 440-729-2486
Free catalog describes herbs, perennials, scented geraniums, ivies, dried herbs, and oils for sale by mail.

The Territorial Seed Company
P.O. Box 158
Cottage Grove, OR 97424-0061
541-942-9547 [F] 888-657-3131
www.territorial-seed.com/home.html
Informative catalog lists gourmet herbs and vegetables with cultural information, old-fashioned flowers, garden supplies, and books.

Thompson & Morgan, Inc.
P.O. Box 1308
Jackson, NJ 08527-0308
800-274-7333 [F] 888-466-4769
www.thompson-morgan.com
Free color catalog of the most popular herb, vegetable, and ornamental seeds available by mail order.

The Thyme Garden Herb Company
20546 Alsea Hwy.
Alsea, OR 97324
541-487-8671
www.thymegarden.com
Catalog ($2.00) lists herb seeds and plants, dried herbs, seasonings, and tea blends sold by mail.

Well Sweep Herb Farm
205 Mount Bethel Rd.
Port Murray, NJ 07865
908-852-5390
www.wellsweep.com
Online catalog or free print catalog lists herb plants and perennials.

SUGGESTED READING

Bailey, Liberty Hyde. *Hortus Third: A Concise Dictionary of Plants Cultivated in the United States and Canada.* Indianapolis, IN: Hungry Minds, Inc., 1976.

Boxer, Arabella, et al. *The Encyclopedia of Herbs, Spices, and Flavorings.* New York: Crescent Books, 1984.

Brown, Deni. *New Encyclopedia of Herbs and Their Uses.* New York: DK Publishing, 2001.

Culpeper, Nicholas. *Culpeper's Complete Herbal: A Book of Natural Remedies of Ancient Ills.* London: W. Foulsham & Company Ltd., [19–].

Cunningham, Scott. *Cunningham's Encyclopedia of Magical Herbs,* Llewellyn's Sourcebook Series. St. Paul, MN: Llewellyn Publications, 1985.

Day, Avanelle. *The Spice Cookbook.* New York: Grossett & Dunlap, 1968.

Ellacombe, Henry N. *The Plant-Lore & Garden-Craft of Shakespeare,* 2nd ed. New York: AMS Press, 1973.

Gerard, John. *Gerard's Herbal: John Gerard's Historie of Plants.* Collingdale, PA: DIANE Publishing Co., 2000.

Gordon, Jean. *The Art of Cooking with Roses.* New York: Crescent Books, 1971.

Grieve, M. A. *Modern Herbal: The Medicinal, Culinary, Cosmetic and Economic Properties, Cultivation and Folk Lore of Herbs, Grasses, Fungi Shrubs and Trees.* New York: Dover Publications, 1971.

Hanle, Zack. *Cooking with Flowers.* New York: Irena Chalmers Cookbooks, 1971.

Hemphill, Ian. *The Herb & Spice Bible: A Cook's Guide.* Ontario, Canada: Robert Rose Inc.; Firefly Books, 2002.

Herb Companion. Loveland, CO: Interweave Press. Bi-monthly magazine.

Herb Quarterly. Boiling Spring, PA: Long Mountain Press.

Herbst, Sharon Tyler. *New Food Lover's Companion: Comprehensive Definitions of Over 3000 Food, Wine and Culinary Terms,* Barrons Educational Series, 2001.

Houdret, Jessica. *Ultimate Book of Herbs & Herb Gardening.* New York: Lorenz Books; London: Anness Publishing, 1999.

Keller, Mitzie Stuart. *Mysterious Herbs and Roots: Ancient Secrets for Beauty, Health, Magick, Prevention and Youth, 1600 B.C.–1900 A.D.* Culver City, CA: Peace Press, 1978.

Kowalchik, Claire. *Rodale's Illustrated Encyclopedia of Herbs.* St. Emmaus, PA: Rodale Press, 1998.

Lathrop, Norma Jean. *Herbs: How to Select, Grow, and Enjoy Them.* Tucson, AZ: H.P. Books, 1981.

Lehner, Ernst. *Folklore and Symbolism of Flowers, Plants, and Trees.* Holmes, NY: Tudor Publishing, 1960.

McGee, Harold. *On Food and Cooking: The Science and Lore of the Kitchen.* New York: Charles Scribner, 1984.

Northcote, Lady Rosalind. *The Book of Herb Lore,* 2nd ed. New York: Dover Publications, 1971.

Ortiz, Elizabeth Lambert. *Encyclopedia of Herbs, Spices, & Flavorings.* New York: DK Publishing, 1996.

Parkinson, John. *Paradisi in Sole Paradisus Terrestris. Or a Garden of All Sorts of Pleasant Flowers Which Our English Ayre Will Permit to be Noursed. With a Kitchen Garden of All Manner of Herbes, Rootes, & Fruites, for Meate or Sause. Vsed with Vs, and an Orchard of All Sorte of Fruitbearing Trees and Shrubbes Fit.* London: printed by Humphrey Lownes and Robert Young at the sign of the Starre on Bread-street hill, 1629.

———. *Theaetrum Botanicum: The Theater of Plants. Or, an Herball of a Large Extent: Containing Therein a More Ample and Exact History and Declaration of the Physicall Herbs and Plants that are in Other Authours, Encreased by the Accese of Many Hundreds of New, Rare, and Strange Plants from All the Parts of the World.* London: printed by Tho. Cotes, 1640.

Saville, Carole. *Exotic Herbs: A Compendium of Exceptional Culinary Herbs.* New York: Henry Holt & Company, Inc., 1997.

Turner, William. *A New Herbal,* ed. George T. L. Chapman, et al. Cambridge, New York: Cambridge University Press, 1995.

Tusser, Thomas. *One Hundred Good Pointes of Husbandry, Lately Maried onto a Hundreth Good Pointes of Housewifery, New Corrected,* collated and edited by Dorothy Hartley. 1571. Reprint, London: Country Life, Ltd., 1931.

Tyler, Varro. *Tyler's Honest Herbal: A Sensible Guide to the Use of Herbs and Related Remedies.* Binghamton, NY: Haworth Press, 1999.

INDEX

ACKNOWLEDGMENTS

To supplement the recipes I've used over the years in my classes on herbs, I issued an appeal to all of the members of the Huntington community, including staff, volunteers, and scholars, to submit recipes. An overwhelming response ensued but one question remained—which recipes to choose? The recipes needed to be tested, and the testing needed to be organized.

Fortunately, many devoted, talented volunteers agreed to help. Chris Benter, an energetic and delightful woman who has worked on Junior League cookbooks in the past, agreed to co-chair the volunteer committee. She recruited the chapter chairpersons, who were responsible for making sure that the recipes in their chapter were tested, the results recorded, and recommendations made for inclusion in the book. Chris was ably assisted by Penny Kirby, who also worked on other community cookbooks. Penny compiled the recipes, duplicated them for the chapter chairpersons, and kept track of the files. Chris and Penny, as well as each of the chapter chairpersons, deserve my undying thanks for testing, retesting, and adapting the recipes as necessary. Experienced and able cooks, they devoted a great deal of time, energy, and resources to this effort, even though every one of them had other projects and commitments.

Members of the Huntington staff also helped test recipes, and other friends inspired and encouraged me, in addition to sharing and testing recipes.

SHIRLEY KERINS

San Marino, California

Volunteer Cookbook Committee

Co-Chairs
Chris Benter
Penny Kirby

Special Projects
Maria Grant
Alison Sowden

Computer Chair
Ronda Carlson

**Bibliography
and Sources**
Maria Blumberg

**Herb Butters, Sauces,
Pestos, Salsas,
and Marinades**
Betty Medearis
Marge Telleen

Appetizers
Julie Condon
Pam Livingston

**Salads and
Salad Dressings**
Sue Barry
Susan Carrier
Nancy Thomas

Soups
Bobbi Hewins
Nadine Skotheim
Jan Smiley

Breads
Mitty Hollingsworth

Pasta and Pizza
Marion Haines
Marion Pattenson

**Vegetables and
Side Dishes**
Pat Ellison
Judy Martin

Main Courses
Carl Dienst
Warren Johnson
Barbara Knapp

Desserts
Anne Blomstrom
Erika Riley

**Jams, Jellies,
and Beverages**
Diane Martin

Volunteers

These volunteers submitted and tested recipes and helped in a variety of other ways.

Cathy Asher	Bonnie DeWitt	Richard Homet	Anne Meyers	Sherm Telleen
Catherine Babcock	Adella Diaz	Julia Hong	Muriel Newell	Kathleen Thorne-Thomsen
Mimi Beasley	Peggy Dienst	Barbara House	Susanne Orr	Hoby Tottle
Marie Bellotti	Aimee Dozois	Muffy Hunt	Rachel Pastre	Carol Towey
Barbara Bishop	Judith Farrar	Bill Hutchins	Earlymae Payne	Daphne Trager
Dorothy Blakesley	Jim Folsom	Diane Kanner	Laura Perry	Annie Van Dyke
Marilyn Bressler	Yolanda Fontana	Robin Kaplan	Mary Pinola	Carol Viani
Paula Brody	Marilyn Gerich	Peggy Kelly	Monica Pitts	Linnea Warren
Susan Chandler	Kim Gonzalez	Jimmie Kirby	Julie Quinn	Letty Watkins
Frits Claase	Joei Graham	Phoebe Kon	Charlene Saunders	Clifford Wilcox
Nancy Cole	Forrest Grames	Dominique Manning	Celia Sawyer	Sharee Wilkenson
Louise Crawford	Marti Green	Beverly Marksbury	Kenneth Schechter	Angela Wilson
Evie Cutting	Susan Green	Herrrod Marrs	Christine Seller	Mel Wilson
Nadine Danz	Lorie Halstead	Mikie Marsh	Barbara Smith	Debbie Wycoff
Minnie Davis	Megs Herrera	Fay Massey	Deborah Smith	Patty Zuber
		John McHugh	Selena Spurgeon	